THE GREAT

AMERICAN

☆ DESSERT ☆

COOKBOOK

THE GREAT

AMERICAN DESSERT COOKBOOK

By Andrea Chesman and Fran Raboff

The Crossing Press • Freedom, California 95019

The recipes for Apple Dumplings, Apple Pandowdy, and Blueberry Grunt first appeared in *Harrowsmith* (Number 22, July/August 1989).

Library of Congress Cataloging-in-Publication Data

Chesman, Andrea.
        The great American dessert cookbook / Andrea Chesman and Fran
Raboff.
                p.   cm.
        Includes index.
        ISBN 0-89594-438-3   -- ISBN 0-89594-437-5 (pbk.)
        1. Desserts.   I. Raboff, Fran.   II. Title.
TX773. C522 1990
641.8'6--dc20   90-40533
                                                              CIP

We would like to thank Albina Aspell, Ann Aspell, Dorothy Gertz, Andrea Morgante, Lenore Shapiro, Millie Stark, and Florence Warner for the loan of old cookbooks and old family treasures from their recipe files. And our special thanks go to to our families and friends who have lent support and enthusiastic response to the making of this book.

Contents

☆☆☆☆☆☆☆☆☆☆☆

Of all the books produced since the remote ages by human talents and industry, those only that treat of cooking are, from a moral point of view, above suspicion. The intention of every other piece of prose may be discussed and even mistrusted, but the purpose of a cookery book is one and unmistakable. Its object can conceivably be no other than to increase the happiness of mankind.

Joseph Conrad

Introduction

☆ ☆

Here is a collection of truly great American desserts—chocolate layer cakes and blueberry pie, cherry cobbler and apple pandowdy, lemon meringue and chocolate cream pie, strawberry shortcake and grasshopper pie, chocolate chip cookies and gingerbread men, butterscotch pudding and baked apple dumplings. The classics, the originals, the best.

Because when you want a birthday cake, nothing but a tall devil's food cake will do. And when strawberries are finally available locally, your first impulse is to make strawberry shortcake. Likewise, gingerbread cheers up a friend laid up with a broken leg, and a creamy rice pudding soothes the soul after a hard week at work. We all have eaten and enjoyed the elaborate restaurant desserts created by trained pastry chefs, but we love the good old, old-fashioned desserts best. That is what this book is about.

One of the heirloom recipes we tested for this book was an old recipe for chocolate cake that came from a Hershey's cocoa tin. At one time or another, probably half the households in this country ate that cake. The saying may be "As American as apple pie," but the truth of the matter is that apple pie was invented in

England. What America can proudly claim as its own is the layer cake, and the chocolate layer cake may be its best example.

This is because baking powder, the leavening agent in layer cakes, was an American invention. Before the days of baking powder, cakes were leavened with eggs, sometimes with yeast. The egg cakes required a phenomenal amount of beating. Old recipes can be found that begin with "Separate your eggs and beat for five hours . . ." Tall cakes were layers of baked sponge cake, sandwiched with sweetened creams and jellies.

As early as the Middle Ages, professional bakers knew that baked goods could be leavened with alkaline salts. They made something called pearl ash from refined wood ash and from a type of Spanish seaweed. In Northern Europe, bakers used the refined salts from the ash of deer antlers.

In the colonies, the Indians added wood ash to their cornmeal cakes to sweeten the batter. (The wood ash also added essential amino acids to the corn, making it a complete protein.) The colonists took the innovation a step further by using sour milk to moisten the corn cakes. When the acid of the sour milk reacted with the alkaline wood ash, bubbles of carbon dioxide were formed, which made the cakes lighter. The colonists called the wood ash potash, and later changed the name to pearl ash. By the 1790s, America was shipping tons of pearl ash to Europe.

Pearl ash was eventually replaced by saleratus, or baking soda, which was chemically similar. Both still required an acid to work — sour milk, buttermilk, chocolate, molasses. Saleratus was sold in little envelopes with recipes printed on the back. Imagine what a vast improvement in the housewife's life saleratus represented! She could make bread without long rising times, cakes without hours of beating eggs.

The ready adoption of saleratus was made possible by the development of the iron cooking range. These cookstoves provided the intense heat needed for the chemical activation of saleratus, something that open fireplaces couldn't provide. So the iron cookstove lightened the housewives' care load in several ways. Besides freeing the cook from the slow methods of hearth cookery, it enabled her to utilize time-saving ingredients, such as saleratus and baking soda.

Then it was discovered that baking soda plus cream of tartar could be used with a sweet milk batter. And thus began the baking powder industry and our American layer cakes.

Pies were ever a standard in the American colonies. What better way to use the dried fruits, the moldy apples, the abundance of fresh summer berries, than to encase them in a crust made of flour and lard?

From the South comes some of our most beloved American pies. Sure, apple pie is a favorite—on both sides of the Atlantic—but from the South comes pecan pies, chess pies, black bottom pies, and key lime pies, to name a few. That the South was the center of pastry innovations is explained in part by the fact that white sugar was more plentiful in the South, while the rest of the country still relied on the more heavily flavored molasses and maple syrup. Skillful slave cooks contributed significantly to this period of culinary development. Also, after the Civil War, a shortage of dairy cows led to the introduction of canned condensed milk—the creamy base for key lime pies and countless other chiffon pies. Pie, any time of the day, even for breakfast, became the rage in the 1800s.

The history of American desserts, indeed American cooking, is a rich one. It begins with English cookery, brought over by the stern Puritans of New England, the industrious Quakers of Pennsylvania, and the prosperous colonists of Virginia. In the far North and again in the South, French colonists also exerted a profound influence. From these beginnings come our deep-dish fruit pies and cobblers, our whimsically named fools, and sweet and creamy puddings.

A second wave of immigration brought Scotch-Irish, German, and Dutch cooking. Meanwhile the African slaves can be

credited with bringing both new foods and new techniques to what was to become American cooking. Into this rich legacy came the American foods—cornmeal, maple syrup, and an abundance of fruits and nuts.

The very first American cookbook, Eliza Smith's *The Compleat Housewife,* was printed in Williamsburg, Virginia, in 1742 and reprinted there in 1752, and reprinted again in New York in 1764. American by imprint only, the book was a best-seller in England. A few more books followed, but these cookbooks continued to reflect the culinary arts of England.

We know, however, from diaries and hand-written "receipt" books that a distinctive American cuisine was beginning to emerge. New Englanders were eating chowder, Indian pudding, and baked beans sweetened with molasses and maple syrup; Southerners were enjoying beaten biscuits and discovering tomatoes and okra. It wasn't until 1796 that these new foods and dishes were committed to print—in Amelia Simmons' *American Cookery*, which was published in Hartford, Connecticut.

Simmons described herself as an American orphan, suggesting that those who aren't fortunate enough to be privy to the cooking secrets of mother and grandmother must rely on the printed word. And so began, perhaps, the whole tradition of American self-help books.

Mothers and grandmothers would have been a help in those days, even when the aid of a cookbook was available. Recipes in those early cookbooks disdained measures and timings. All was approximate, as ingredients and temperatures in fireplaces and cookstove ovens were hardly standardized.

Small wonder, then, that some of our favorite and most enduring desserts are the simplest—layers of fruit and biscuit, fruit in a pastry shell, cookies. Our culinary forebears invented recipes that fit the larder—they had no choice but to bake with what was always at hand—flour, sugar, butter, eggs, and fruit—

fresh and preserved. To make things more interesting, they gave their creations whimsical names, like snickerdoodles, grunts, slumps, buckles, dowdies. Not all names can be explained. But all are meant to be enjoyed now, just as much as they were when grandmother and great-grandmother and great-great-grandmother made them.

"A thousand good cooks taught me these wonderful uses for condensed milk"

MILDRED MADDOCKS BENTLEY

Former Director of Good Housekeeping Institute and world-known consultant on home economic subjects, tells what she learned from correspondence with enthusiastic women—and of her own confirming tests.

"WHERE did you *ever* learn to make so many good things with Condensed Milk?" asked an old friend of mine the other day.

"From a correspondence course," I laughed. Then, seeing her puzzled expression, I explained, "Correspondence with the best cooking teachers in the world—everyday practical housewives, like yourself."

"It was *their* letters that first piqued my curiosity to learn more about Condensed Milk. Of course I'd already discovered its advantages in coffee. But *why* was it so much better for certain cooking than the old method of using plain milk and sugar?

"I went for my answer straight to those women who used Condensed Milk for cooking. They not only *told* me about the dishes they made with it, but actually let me *taste* some of them.

"I asked for the recipes, unblushingly—hurried back home, ordered some Borden's Eagle Brand Condensed Milk, and began experiments at once in my own kitchen to discover the secret.

"It was simply this. Condensed Milk is full-cream milk with part of the water removed, making it *doubly* rich. Then sugar is blended with the milk—*cooked* with it—so thoroughly that it gives a smooth, rich *blended* consistency to your cooking—and to your coffee—which you can get in no other way.

"Just try the following recipes for the dishes illustrated—special favorites with my correspondents—and you'll appreciate what I mean. A thousand good cooks taught me these wonderful uses for Condensed Milk.

"If you're wondering how to make the luscious Spanish Cream and Fudge illustrated here, you can best satisfy your curiosity by sending for a copy of my book, *Milk and its Place in Good Cookery*. This is more than just a recipe book for Condensed Milk dishes. It's a complete 'encyclopedia' on Milk. You'll find in it a wealth of milk information to help you in planning and preparing meals—with hundreds of tested recipes using all forms of milk. Any woman who is interested, may secure a free copy of this book by writing to the Borden Company, 401 Borden Building, 350 Madison Ave., New York.

"In the meantime order some Eagle Brand Condensed Milk—one of the several Borden brands—and treat your family to it in coffee and in some of these dishes."

CONDENSED MILK CHOCOLATE FROSTING

2 squares unsweetened chocolate · ½ cup Borden's Condensed Milk
1 tablespoon butter · 1 teaspoon vanilla

Break chocolate in small pieces, melt with butter over hot water. Blend with condensed milk and flavoring. Beat until thick enough to spread between layers and on top of cake.

RICE PUDDING

½ cup rice · ½ teaspoon salt
¾ cup Borden's Condensed Milk · 1 tablespoon butter
2½ cups water · 2 eggs, slightly beaten
Rind of one-half lemon · ½ cup seeded raisins (may be omitted)
thinly sliced

Wash rice thoroughly, cover with cold water, soak one hour, drain. Dilute milk with cold water, stirring well to blend. Add rice, salt and lemon rind, cook in a double boiler until rice is tender and milk nearly absorbed. Remove lemon rind, stir in eggs and butter. Cook slowly five minutes longer. Add raisins, pour into a buttered pudding dish, bake in a moderate oven twenty minutes.

CARAMEL PUDDING
(the famous dessert that makes itself)

Place unopened can of Borden's Condensed Milk in a kettle of boiling water and simmer for two and a half hours, being careful not to let the kettle boil dry. Remove can, cool, and chill. Remove top of can, cutting along the side of the can—not the top—so that the contents may be removed whole; place on a serving dish, garnish with broken nut meats and whipped cream. To serve individually, cut in slices, garnish with nut meats and whipped cream—or use plain unsweetened cream, with or without garnish.

Mildred Maddocks Bentley

Borden's
EAGLE BRAND CONDENSED MILK

FULL CREAM COUNTRY MILK AND SUGAR

Always the right milk for the right purpose.

Borden's Eagle Brand—the finest grade of condensed milk. For coffee and sweetened cooking. Famous for infants. *Borden's Other Brands Condensed Milk*—less rich, in smaller cans. For household use. *Borden's Evaporated Milk*—for unsweetened cooking. *Borden's Malted Milk*—a food-beverage, plain or chocolate flavor.

Cakes

☆ ☆

Devil's Food Cake

☆ ☆ ☆ ☆ ☆ ☆ ☆ ☆ ☆ ☆ ☆ ☆ ☆ ☆ ☆ ☆ ☆ ☆ ☆ ☆

2½ cups sifted all-purpose unbleached flour
⅔ cup unsweetened cocoa
1 tablespoon baking soda
¼ teaspoon salt
½ cup butter, at room temperature
1⅔ cups sugar
5 eggs
1⅓ cups buttermilk or plain yogurt
1 teaspoon vanilla extract
Fudge Frosting (page 54)

How did this cake earn its name? Was it that the cake was so rich, it tasted like sin to our grandmothers? Some writers hold that theory and suggest that some wag named devil's food cake to contrast with angel food cake, an earlier, all-white creation. Another theory explains that devil's food is a cake leavened by baking soda, and when the soda interacts with cocoa, it gives a reddish tint to the cake, hence the association with the devil. Some recipes in the '50s called for adding an entire bottle of red food coloring to the batter to enhance the red tint. We have made the cake with and without the food coloring and think the color change is subtle and not worth the bother.

☆ ☆ ☆

Preheat the oven to 350° F. Grease and flour two 9-inch round cake pans. Line the bottoms with parchment or waxed paper, grease again, then sprinkle with flour to coat completely. Shake out any excess flour. Set aside.

Sift together the flour, cocoa, baking soda, and salt. Set aside.

In a large mixing bowl, beat the butter until creamy, then gradually add the sugar and beat until fluffy. Add the eggs, one at a time, beating well after each addition.

Add the flour mixture to the egg mixture alternately with the buttermilk, and beat until smooth. Mix in the vanilla. Pour the batter into the prepared pans.

Bake for 30 to 35 minutes, or until a cake tester inserted into the center of the cake comes out clean. Cool on wire racks for about 10 minutes. Remove the cakes from the pans and continue to cool on wire racks. Frost with Fudge Frosting when completely cool.

YIELD: 10 TO 12 SERVINGS

Cake batters that use baking soda for leavening require an acid ingredient to work. When heat is applied, the acid activates the baking soda, causing it to release bubbles of carbon dioxide, which raise the cake. The acid can be supplied by buttermilk, yogurt, or sour milk, inter-changeably. Butter-milk and yogurt are both dairy products made by culturing sweet milk with friendly bacteria. Sour milk is made at home by adding 1 teaspoon of lemon juice or vinegar to 1 cup of milk at room temperature. Then it is set aside for 15 minutes.

Chocolate Layer Cake

☆☆☆☆☆☆☆☆☆☆☆☆☆☆☆☆☆☆☆☆☆☆☆

3 ounces unsweetened
   chocolate
2 cups sifted cake flour
1 teaspoon baking soda
½ teaspoon salt
6 tablespoons butter,
   at room temperature
1½ cups sugar
2 eggs
1 teaspoon vanilla extract
½ cup sour cream
¾ cup milk
Chocolate Frosting
   (page 55)
Garnish: 8 walnut halves
   (optional)

Theobroma, food of the gods, that's how chocolate is known in Latin. Can a birthday party be complete without a chocolate layer cake? This is a dark moist cake with a tender texture.

Preheat the oven to 350° F. Lightly grease two 8-inch round layer cake pans. Line the bottoms with parchment or waxed paper, grease again, then sprinkle with flour to coat completely. Shake out any excess flour. Set aside.

Melt the chocolate over very low heat, stirring until smooth. Set aside to cool.

Sift together the flour, baking soda, and salt. Set aside.

In a large mixing bowl, beat the butter until creamy, then gradually add the sugar, beating until fluffy. Add the eggs, one at a time, beating well after each addition. Blend in the melted chocolate and vanilla. Add the dry ingredients alternately with the sour cream and milk, mixing just until the batter is smooth and blended. Spoon the batter into the prepared pans.

Bake for 30 to 35 minutes, or until a cake tester inserted in the center of cake comes out clean. Cool on wire racks for about 10 minutes. Remove the cakes from the pans and continue to cool on wire racks. Frost with Chocolate Frosting when completely cool. Garnish with the walnut halves, if desired.

YIELD: 8 SERVINGS

HOW TO MAKE A GREAT CAKE

Take forty eggs and divide the whites from the yolks, and beat them to a froth.

Then work four pounds of butter to a cream, and put the whites of the eggs to it, a tablespoonful at a time, until it is well worked.

Then put four pounds of sugar, finely powdered, to it in the same manner.

Then put in the yolks of eggs and five pounds of flour and five pounds of fruit.

Two hours will bake it.

Add to it one-half an ounce of mace, one nutmeg, one-half pint of wine and some French brandy.

This was made by Martha Custis for her grandmama.

From Mrs. Colquitt's *Savannah Cook Book;* the recipe itself was copied from an older manuscript dated Mt. Vernon, 1781.

erman Chocolate Cake

☆ ☆

**6 ounces dark sweet choco-
   late, cut into small pieces**
½ cup water
2⅓ cups sifted cake flour
1 teaspoon baking soda
½ teaspoon salt
**1 cup butter or margarine,
   at room temperature**
1½ cups sugar
4 egg yolks
1 teaspoon vanilla extract
1 cup buttermilk or yogurt
**4 egg whites, at room
   temperature**
¼ teaspoon cream of tartar
¼ cup sugar
**Coconut Pecan Frosting
   (page 60)**

One would think that this cake has its origins in Germany, or with German settlers in Pennsylvania or the Midwest, but it isn't so. It seems that when Walter Baker, grandson of the founder of Baker's Chocolate, teamed up with a gentleman named German, they created a sweet baking chocolate, such as the one used here. This cake owes its name to the "German" chocolate that is used in the recipe. The original recipe was printed on a box of German sweet chocolate.

Although you can use just about any frosting for this cake, the Coconut Pecan Frosting is traditional.

Preheat the oven to 350° F. Lightly grease three 9-inch round layer cake pans. Line the bottoms with parchment or waxed paper, grease again, and then sprinkle with flour to coat completely. Shake out any excess flour. Set aside.

Combine the chocolate and water and melt over very low heat, stirring until smooth. Set aside to cool.

Sift together the flour, baking soda, and salt. Set aside.

In a large mixing bowl, beat the butter until creamy. Gradually add the 1½ cups sugar, beating until fluffy. Add the egg yolks, one at a time, beating well after each addition. Blend in the melted chocolate and vanilla. Add the dry ingredients alternately with the buttermilk, mixing just until the batter is smooth and blended.

In another bowl, beat the egg whites until foamy, add the cream of tartar, and beat until soft peaks form. Add the remaining ¼ cup sugar gradually, and beat until stiff but not dry. The egg whites should hold their shape and remain moist. Stir one-quarter of the egg whites into the batter, then gently fold in the remainder. Spoon the batter into the prepared pans.

Bake for 30 to 35 minutes, or until a cake tester inserted in the center of cake comes out clean. Cool on wire racks for 10 minutes. Remove the cakes from the pans and continue to cool on wire racks. Frost with Coconut Pecan Frosting when completely cool.

YIELD: 10 TO 12 SERVINGS

"Let all things be done decently and in order" and the first thing to put in order when you are going to bake is yourself. Secure the hair in a net or other covering, to prevent any from falling, and brush the shoulders and back to be sure none are lodged there and might blow off; make the hands and fingernails clean, roll the sleeves up above the elbows, and put on a large clean apron. Clean the kitchen table of utensils and everything not needed, and provide everything that will be needed until the cake is baked, not forgetting even the broom-splints previously picked off a new broom and laid away carefully in a little box. (A knitting needle may be kept for testing cake instead of splints.)

If it is warm weather, place the eggs in cold water, and let stand for a few minutes, as they will then make a finer froth; and be sure they are fresh, as they will not make a stiff froth from any amount of beating if old. The cake-tins should be prepared before the cake, when baking powder is used, as it effervesces but once, and there should be no delay in baking, as the mixture should be made firm by the heat, while the effervescing process is going on.

Mrs. Florence K. Stanton, *The Practical Housekeeper* (Philadelphia: Keeler & Kirkpatrick, 1898).

Gold Cake

☆ ☆ ☆ ☆ ☆ ☆ ☆ ☆ ☆ ☆ ☆ ☆

1¾ cups sifted cake flour
2 teaspoons baking powder
¼ teaspoon salt
½ cup butter, at room
    temperature
1 cup sugar
1 teaspoon orange zest
1 teaspoon orange juice
    concentrate, at room
    temperature, or ½ tea-
    spoon orange extract
8 egg yolks (about ½ cup)
½ cup milk
Orange Frosting (page 59),
    Chocolate Frosting (page
    55), or Fudge Frosting
    (page 54)

This is the yellow cake that simply doesn't come out of a box. We give the cake a suggestion of orange flavor. You can highlight the traces of orange with a tangy orange frosting, or, if you hate to miss an opportunity for chocolate, frost with your favorite chocolate frosting. Fresh orange segments arranged in a sunburst pattern make a lovely garnish.

Preheat the oven to 350° F. Lightly grease two 8-inch round layer cake pans. Line the bottoms with parchment or waxed paper. Grease again, then sprinkle with flour to coat completely. Shake out the excess flour.

Sift together the flour, baking powder, and salt. Set aside.

In a large mixing bowl, beat the butter until creamy, then gradually add the sugar, orange zest, and orange juice concentrate, beating until fluffy.

Beat the egg yolks in a small bowl until thick and lemon colored and combine with the butter mixture. If you are using an electric mixer, add the egg yolks to the butter mixture one at a time, beating thoroughly after each addition.

Add about a quarter of the dry ingredients to the creamed mixture, beating until blended, then add a third of the milk. Repeat the procedure, alternating with the flour and milk, ending with the flour. Mix just until batter is smooth and blended. Divide the batter between the prepared pans.

Bake for 25 to 30 minutes, or until a cake tester inserted in center of cake comes out clean. Cool on wire racks for about 10 minutes. Remove the cakes from the pans and continue to cool. Frost when completely cool.

YIELD: 8 SERVINGS

Coconuts grow in clusters on giant palm trees. They are harvested when their outer husks are green, their shells pliable, and their flesh soft and moist. By the time a coconut arrives in your local supermarket, the shell is dark, its flesh thick, and a great deal of the coconut water—the thin white liquid present in the center of the unripe nut—will have been absorbed into the flesh. When you buy a coconut, feel for a heavy one—the heavier the nut, the juicier it will be.

The flavor of fresh coconut is far superior to the dried packaged flakes. To prepare a fresh coconut: Pierce two of the eyes with a strong, sharp instrument, such as a metal skewer. Shake out the juice. Smell it for rancidity. If it tastes and smells fresh, serve it in a drink; otherwise discard the juice. The flesh will be fine regardless of the state of the milk.

Bake the empty nut in a 400° F. oven for 15 minutes. Lay the hot nut on a table or counter and give it a sharp blow with a hammer right on the center of the shell. It will break cleanly in two. Pare away the brown skin with a sharp knife and grate the white flesh with a food processor.

To make coconut milk, mix fresh grated coconut with boiling water and then squeeze the liquid from the coconut shreds. To make coconut cream, simply use less water, or you can skim the cream from coconut milk that has been left to stand for a long time.

Coconut Cake

☆☆☆☆☆☆☆☆☆☆☆☆☆☆☆

Cake

3½ cups sifted all-purpose
   unbleached flour
5 teaspoons baking powder
1¾ cups sugar
1½ teaspoons salt
1 cup flaked sweetened
   coconut
1⅓ cups milk
6 egg whites, at room
   temperature
1 teaspoon cream of tartar
½ cup butter, at room
   temperature
½ cup solid white vegetable
   shortening
1½ teaspoons coconut
   extract
1½ teaspoons lemon or
   orange extract

Buttercream Frosting

1 cup sweetened flaked
   coconut
½ cup unsalted butter,
   at room temperature
1 pound confectioners sugar,
   sifted
Pinch salt
3 to 4 tablespoons half-and-
   half or light cream
1 teaspoon lemon, orange,
   or vanilla extract
1 ounce unsweetened
   chocolate, melted

We are among those who believe that every good cake deserves a little chocolate. So this snowy white cake is filled with a chocolate buttercream between the layers. Billowy clouds of lemony buttercream and toasted coconut make a luscious topping.

☆ ☆ ☆

Preheat the oven to 350° F. Grease and flour two 9-inch cake pans. Line the bottoms with parchment or waxed paper, grease again, then sprinkle with flour to coat completely. Shake out any excess flour. Set aside.

Sift together the flour, baking powder, sugar, and salt into a medium-size mixing bowl. Stir in the coconut.

In another bowl, combine the milk, egg whites, and cream of tartar. Beat for about 1 minute.

In a large mixing bowl, cream together the butter and shortening until light and fluffy. Add one-third of the flour mixture and one-third of the egg whites. Beat until well blended. Continue adding the flour and egg whites in thirds, until all is combined. Add the extracts and beat for about 1 minute, until well combined. Pour the batter into the prepared cake pans and smooth the tops.

Bake for 25 to 35 minutes, or until a tester inserted into the center comes out clean. Cool on wire racks for about 10 minutes. Remove from the pans and continue to cool on wire racks. Frost when completely cool.

Buttercream Frosting

Spread the coconut on a baking sheet and toast in a 300° F. oven for about 10 minutes. Watch carefully and shake the pan from time to time. Once the coconut begins browning, it will scorch quite easily. Remove from the hot pan and set aside to cool.

Whip the butter with an electric mixer until light and fluffy. Add half the sugar and the salt and beat until combined. Add the remaining sugar, and 3 tablespoons half-and-half. Beat until very smooth, adding more half-and-half as needed for a good spreading consistency.

Remove about three-quarters of the buttercream to a bowl. Mix in the lemon, orange, or vanilla flavoring and set aside. To the remaining buttercream, whip in the melted chocolate until smooth.

Spread the chocolate buttercream between the two cake layers. Cover the top and sides with the white buttercream, swirling the frosting to make swirls and peaks. Sprinkle the toasted coconut on top.

YIELD: 10 TO 12 SERVINGS

Banana Cake

☆ ☆ ☆ ☆ ☆ ☆ ☆ ☆ ☆ ☆ ☆ ☆ ☆

2 cups sifted all-purpose
  unbleached flour
1 teaspoon baking powder
1 teaspoon baking soda
½ teaspoon salt
⅛ teaspoon nutmeg
½ cup butter, margarine,
  or shortening, at room
  temperature
1½ cups sugar
2 eggs
1 teaspoon vanilla extract
1¼ cups mashed ripe
  bananas
⅔ cup buttermilk or yogurt
½ cups toasted chopped
  walnuts (optional)
Sea Foam Frosting (page 61)
  or Chocolate Frosting
  (page 55)

Before man, there were bananas. The Koran says the forbidden fruit in the Garden of Eden was a banana, not an apple. Alexander the Great found the wise men of India eating bananas when he crossed the Indus in 327 B.C., hence the banana's botanical name, *Musa sapientum,* which means "of the wise muse."

☆ ☆ ☆

Preheat the oven to 350° F. Lightly grease two 9-inch round layer cake pans. Line the bottoms with parchment or waxed paper, grease again, then sprinkle with flour to coat completely. Shake out any excess flour. Set aside.

Sift together the flour, baking powder, baking soda, salt, and nutmeg. Set aside.

In a large mixing bowl, beat the butter until creamy, then gradually add the sugar, beating until fluffy. Add the eggs, one at a time, beating well after each addition. Add the vanilla. Add the dry ingredients alternately with the bananas and buttermilk, mixing just until batter is smooth and blended. Fold in the chopped nuts. Spoon the batter into the prepared pans.

Bake for 25 to 30 minutes, or until a cake tester inserted in the center of cake comes out clean. Cool on wire racks for about 10 minutes. Remove the cakes from the pans and continue to cool. Frost when completely cool.

YIELD: 10 TO 12 SERVINGS

WHAT BETTER GIFT?

A WHOLE OR HALF BARREL
King Arthur Flour

A Trim Package
Sensible ~ Elegant ~ Valuable

Spice Cake

☆ ☆ ☆ ☆ ☆ ☆ ☆ ☆ ☆ ☆ ☆

Spice Cake

2¼ cups sifted all-purpose
    unbleached flour
1½ teaspoons baking powder
1 teaspoon baking soda
½ teaspoon salt
1½ teaspoons cinnamon
½ teaspoon ground ginger
½ teaspoon nutmeg
¼ teaspoon ground cloves
¼ teaspoon allspice
½ cup butter, margarine, or
    vegetable shortening, at
    room temperature
1 cup white sugar
½ cup firmly packed dark
    brown sugar
2 eggs
1 teaspoon vanilla extract
1 cup buttermilk, yogurt, or
    sour milk

Coffee Whipped Cream

1 cup heavy whipping cream
1 tablespoon instant coffee
    powder
¼ cup sifted confectioners
    sugar
½ teaspoon vanilla extract

A cup of cappuccino and a frosty fall afternoon do justice to this moist, light spice cake. The coffee-flavored whipped cream is just the right complement to the lively spices.

☆ ☆ ☆

Preheat the oven to 350° F. Lightly grease two 8-inch round layer cake pans. Line the bottoms with parchment or waxed paper. Grease again, then sprinkle with flour to coat completely. Shake out any excess flour. Set aside.

Sift together the flour, baking powder, baking soda, salt, cinnamon, ginger, nutmeg, cloves, and allspice. Set aside.

In a large mixing bowl, beat the butter until creamy, then gradually add the sugars, beating until fluffy. Add the eggs, one at a time, beating well after each addition. Add the vanilla. Add the dry ingredients alternately with the buttermilk, mixing just until the batter is smooth and blended. Divide the batter between the prepared pans.

Bake for 30 minutes, or until a cake tester inserted in the center of the cake comes out clean. Cool on wire racks for about 10 minutes. Remove the cakes from the pans and continue to cool. Frost with the Coffee Whipped Cream when completely cool.

Note: To make sour milk: Add 1 teaspoon of lemon juice or vinegar to 1 cup of milk (at room temperature). Set aside for 15 minutes.

Coffee Whipped Cream

In a bowl, combine the whipping cream and coffee powder. Chill for 15 minutes. Beat until soft peaks form. Add the confectioners sugar and vanilla and beat until stiff. Spread between the layers and over the top and sides of the cake. Keep the frosted cake refrigerated.

YIELD: 8 SERVINGS

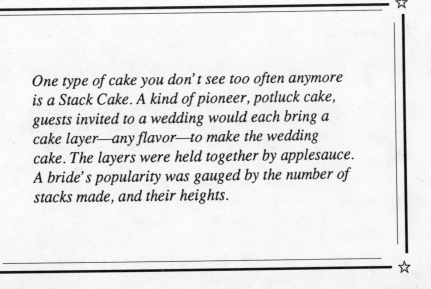

One type of cake you don't see too often anymore is a Stack Cake. A kind of pioneer, potluck cake, guests invited to a wedding would each bring a cake layer—any flavor—to make the wedding cake. The layers were held together by applesauce. A bride's popularity was gauged by the number of stacks made, and their heights.

Boston Cream Pie

☆☆☆☆☆☆☆☆☆☆☆☆☆☆☆☆☆☆☆☆

Cake Layer

1 cup sifted flour
1 teaspoon baking powder
¼ teaspoon salt
2 eggs, at room temperature
1 cup sugar
1¼ teaspoons vanilla extract
1 tablespoon butter
½ cup hot milk

Pastry Cream Filling

¼ cup sugar
2½ tablespoons all-purpose
    unbleached flour
¼ teaspoon salt
1 cup hot (not boiling) milk
    or half-and-half
3 egg yolks, lightly beaten
1 teaspoon vanilla extract
1 tablespoon butter, cut into
    small pieces

Chocolate Glaze

⅔ cup (4 ounces) semi-sweet
    chocolate chips
3 tablespoons milk
1 tablespoon butter
1 cup sifted confectioners
    sugar
1 teaspoon vanilla extract

How did a dessert that is so clearly a cake come to be named a pie? No one seems to know. What is known is that Boston cream pie was on the menu of the famed Parker House in Boston from the time it opened its doors in 1856, but it was originally called a Parker House chocolate pie. Parker House really shouldn't get the credit for inventing this delectable dessert, only for adding the chocolate glaze topping. Cream cakes, or pudding-cake pies, cakes with a cream filling between the layers, do exist in earlier cookbooks, as does the Washington pie, a cake similar to Boston cream pie, but filled with raspberry jam instead of vanilla pudding.

☆ ☆ ☆

To make the cake, preheat the oven to 350° F. Lightly grease two 8-inch round layer cake pans. Line the bottoms of the pans with parchment or waxed paper, grease again, then sprinkle with flour to coat completely. Shake out any excess flour. Set aside.

Sift together the flour, baking powder, and salt three times and leave it in the sifter. Set aside.

In the large bowl of an electric mixer, beat the eggs for 3 to 4 minutes, until thick and lemon colored. Gradually add the sugar and beat for another 5 minutes (by hand beat for 8 minutes). Add the vanilla, mixing until blended. Melt the butter in the hot milk. Using a rubber spatula, mix in the hot milk, pouring it into the batter all at once.

Sift the flour into the mixture, gradually folding it in at the same time. The folding in of the milk and dry ingredients should only take about 1 minute. The batter will be thin. Divide the batter between the prepared pans.

Bake for 20 to 25 minutes, or until a cake tester inserted in center of cake comes out clean. Cool on wire racks for about 10 minutes. Remove the cakes from the pans and continue to cool. Prepare the Pastry Cream Filling. When cooled and chilled, spread the pastry cream between the cake layers. Then spread the chocolate glaze over the top cake layer. Allow the glaze to set for 2 hours before serving.

Pastry Cream Filling

In a heavy-bottomed saucepan, combine the sugar, flour, and salt. Add the hot milk gradually, stirring constantly with a wire whisk to remove any lumps. Cook over medium high heat, stirring constantly until bubbly. Cook and stir for 2 minutes, until it begins to thicken. Remove from the heat.

Stir a few teaspoonfuls of the hot mixture at a time into the egg yolks, beating constantly until well blended. After combining, return the mixture to the saucepan. Stir and cook for 2 minutes longer, until thick and smooth. Remove from the heat. Add the vanilla. Gradually stir in the butter. Cover the surface of the pastry cream with plastic. When the pastry cream is cool, chill in the refrigerator.

Chocolate Glaze

In a small saucepan, combine the chocolate chips, milk, and butter. Cook over very low heat until melted and smooth. Gradually combine the chocolate mixture with the confectioners sugar. Stir in the vanilla. Cool until thick enough to spread.

YIELD: 8 SERVINGS

Chocolate Marble Cake

☆ ☆

½ cup unsweetened cocoa
¼ cup sugar
¼ cup strong coffee
3 cups sifted cake flour
2 teaspoons baking powder
1 teaspoon baking soda
½ teaspoon salt
¾ cup butter or margarine,
    at room temperature
1¾ cups sugar
1½ teaspoons vanilla extract
4 eggs
1⅔ cups buttermilk or
    yogurt, at room
    temperature
Zest of 1 orange
Garnish: Sifted confectioners
    sugar (optional)

I remember watching my grandmother swirl chocolate batter into marble cake. It seemed the most marvelous trick, that with a flick of her wrist she could create lovely patterns in the cake. Marble cakes—made with molasses, rather than chocolate, are probably the invention of Mennonites from Pennsylvania. The Pennsylvania Dutch were known for their vast range and skill when it came to cooking, and they particularly excelled in dessert making.

☆ ☆ ☆

Preheat the oven to 350° F. Lightly grease and flour a 9-inch tube or bundt pan. Set aside.

In a medium-size bowl, mix the cocoa and the ¼ cup sugar. Add the coffee gradually and stir until blended. Set aside.

Sift together the flour, baking powder, baking soda, and salt. Set aside.

In a large mixing bowl, beat the butter until creamy, then gradually add the remaining 1¾ cups sugar and vanilla, beating until fluffy. Add the eggs, one at a time, beating well after each addition. Add the dry ingredients alternately with the buttermilk, mixing just until the batter is smooth and blended. Remove about one third of the batter and add it to the cocoa mixture, blending well.

To the remaining batter in the mixing bowl, stir in the orange zest.

Using a tablespoon, add alternate spoonfuls of the white and chocolate batters into the prepared baking pan. Swirl a spatula through the batter to give a marble effect.

Bake for 55 to 60 minutes, or until a cake tester inserted in the center of the cake comes out clean. Cool on a wire rack for about 10 minutes. Run a spatula carefully around the sides and center tube of the pan before turning the cake out onto the rack. The cake should cool right side up. Sprinkle with confectioners sugar, if desired, just before serving.

YIELD: 10 TO 12 SERVINGS

Applessauce Cake

☆☆☆☆☆☆☆☆☆☆☆☆☆☆☆☆☆

½ cup raisins
½ cup dried currants
1 tablespoon all-purpose
   unbleached flour
1²/₃ cups sifted all-purpose
   unbleached flour
1 teaspoon baking powder
½ teaspoon baking soda
¼ teaspoon salt
1 teaspoon cinnamon
½ teaspoon nutmeg
½ teaspoon ground cloves
½ cup butter or margarine,
   at room temperature
¾ cup white sugar
½ cup firmly packed dark
   brown sugar
2 eggs
1 teaspoon vanilla extract
1 cup thick applesauce,
   warmed
2 tablespoons milk
Brown Sugar Frosting
   (page 62)
Garnish: Chopped peanuts or
   toasted almonds

One of the pleasures of fall is going to a nearby orchard and picking apples. Depending on whether we pick early or late, we have our choice of Red Delicious, McIntoshes, or Northern Spies. The Spies ripen late, and our fingers are tinged red with the cold by the time we have picked our bushel.

We make a stop at the bin of "drops" for bargain-priced sauce apples, which we cook down, strain, and flavor with cinnamon, no sugar needed. Some of that sauce makes its way into this moist cake.

☆ ☆ ☆

Preheat the oven to 350° F. Lightly grease and flour a 9-inch tube or bundt pan. Set aside.

In a small bowl, toss the raisins and currants with the 1 tablespoon of flour. Set aside.

Sift together the 1²/₃ cups flour, baking powder, baking soda, salt, cinnamon, nutmeg, and cloves. Set aside.

In a large mixing bowl, beat the butter until creamy, then gradually add the sugars, beating until fluffy. Add the eggs, one at a time, beating well after each addition. Add the vanilla. Add the dry ingredients alternately with the warm applesauce and milk, mixing just until batter is smooth and blended. Fold in the raisins and currants. Spoon the batter into the prepared pan.

Bake for 45 to 50 minutes, or until a cake tester inserted in the center of cake comes out clean. Cool on a wire rack for about 10 minutes. Run a spatula carefully around the sides and center tube of the pan before turning the cake out onto the rack. The cake should cool right side up. Frost with the Brown Sugar Frosting when completely cool. Sprinkle with the chopped nuts.

YIELD: 10 TO 12 SERVINGS

*I remember that at one time I saw two of my young mistresses
and some lady visitors eating ginger-cakes, in the yard. At that
time those cakes seemed to me to be absolutely the most tempting and desirable things I had ever seen and then and there
resolved that, if I ever got free, the height of my ambition would
be reached if I could get to the point where I could secure and
eat ginger-cakes in the way I saw those ladies doing.*

Booker T. Washington, *Up From Slavery*, 1901.

Gingerbread

☆☆☆☆☆☆☆☆☆☆☆☆☆☆

1½ cups sifted all-purpose
    unbleached flour
1 teaspoon baking soda
2 teaspoons ground ginger
¾ teaspoon cinnamon
¼ teaspoon ground cloves
¼ teaspoon salt
½ cup butter or margarine, at
    room temperature
¾ cup firmly packed dark
    brown sugar
1 egg, lightly beaten
½ cup dark table molasses
    (not blackstrap)
½ cup boiling hot coffee
Garnish: Confectioners
    sugar (optional)

The first cake I ever made from scratch was a gingerbread. For me it is the quintessential comfort food—wildly appetizing as it bakes and fills the house with the warm scent of ginger, richly satisfying to eat, and a wonderful excuse for whipped cream. It's also delicious served with applesauce or rhubarb sauce and vanilla ice cream.

☆ ☆ ☆

Preheat the oven to 350°F. Lightly grease and flour an 8-inch square pan. Set aside.

Sift together the flour, baking soda, ginger, cinnamon, cloves, and salt. Set aside.

In a bowl, beat the butter until creamy, then gradually add the sugar, beating until fluffy. Add the egg and beat until smooth, then beat in the molasses. Add the dry ingredients alternately with the boiling coffee, mixing until just combined. (The batter will be thin.) Pour into the prepared pan.

Bake for about 35 minutes, or until a cake tester inserted in the center of the cake comes out clean. Cool on a wire rack.

To make a special presentation, you can top the gingerbread with a design made from confectioners sugar. To do so, use a triple thickness of decorative paper doilies. Remove any excess uncut paper. Fasten the doily to the top of the gingerbread with toothpicks or pins. Sprinkle over and around the doily with sifted confectioners sugar. Remove the picks or pins and lift the doily straight up. There should remain a lacy snowflake design of powdered sugar.

YIELD: 6 TO 8 SERVINGS

Gingerbread

Three pounds of flour, a grated nutmeg, two ounces ginger, one pound sugar, three small spoons pearl ash dissolved in cream, one pound butter, four eggs, knead it stiff, shape it to your fancy, bake 15 minutes.

Amelia Simmons, an American Orphan. American Cookery: or the art of Dressing Viands, Fish, Poultry & Vegetables and the best Modes of Making Pastes, Puffs, Pies, Tarts, Puddings, Custards & Preserves and All Kinds of Cakes from the Imperial Plumb to Plain Cake adapted to This Country & All Grades of Life, *1796.*

Carrot Cake

☆☆☆☆☆☆☆☆☆☆☆☆☆

2 cups sifted all-purpose
  unbleached flour
2 teaspoons baking powder
1½ teaspoons baking soda
1 teaspoon salt
1½ teaspoons cinnamon
¼ teaspoon nutmeg
¼ teaspoon allspice
1 cup vegetable oil
1 cup white sugar
¾ cup firmly packed light
  brown sugar
4 eggs, at room temperature
1 tablespoon orange zest
1 teaspoon vanilla extract
3 cups lightly packed, finely
  shredded carrots
8 ounces drained crushed
  pineapple
1 cup toasted chopped
  walnuts
Cream Cheese Frosting
  (page 63)
Garnish: Toasted coconut
  (optional)

Those who scoffed at seed eaters and granola crunchers were forced to rethink their prejudices when it came to carrot cake. And why did carrot cake become the standard bearer of health food aficionados? It could have been because the moist cake stands up even to the assault of whole wheat, or perhaps because it is packed with fiber and vitamins and low in animal fats. Perhaps people adopted it because the recipe was so often foolproof and lent itself to multiplication for huge wedding cakes. Or, perhaps, carrot cake became so universally popular because it tastes so good.

☆ ☆ ☆

Preheat the oven to 350° F. Lightly grease and flour a 9-inch by 13-inch baking pan. Set aside.

Sift together the flour, baking powder, baking soda, salt, cinnamon, nutmeg, and allspice. Set aside.

In a mixing bowl, beat the oil and sugars until thoroughly combined. Add the eggs, one at a time, beating well after each addition. Add the orange zest and vanilla; continue beating until fluffy. Gradually add the dry ingredients, mixing just until the batter is smooth and blended. Fold in the carrots, pineapple, and walnuts. Spoon into the prepared pan.

Bake for 35 minutes, or until a cake tester inserted in the center of the cake comes out clean. Cool on a wire rack for about 10 minutes. Remove the cake from the pan and continue to cool. Frost with Cream Cheese Frosting when completely cool. Or cool and frost in the pan. Sprinkle with toasted coconut, if desired.

YIELD: 12 TO 16 SERVINGS

Black walnuts are native to the eastern part of the United States, while English walnuts originated in Persia. Black walnuts are much more strongly flavored than English walnuts, and some may prefer to use half and half in their recipes. Toasting English walnuts definitely enhances their flavor.

Black Walnut Cake

☆ ☆ ☆ ☆ ☆ ☆ ☆ ☆ ☆ ☆ ☆ ☆ ☆ ☆ ☆ ☆ ☆ ☆ ☆

2¾ cups sifted cake flour
2½ teaspoons baking powder
¾ teaspoon salt
⅔ cup butter or margarine, at
   room temperature
1 cup white sugar
⅔ cup firmly packed dark
   brown sugar
3 eggs
1 teaspoon vanilla extract
1 cup milk
1½ cups finely chopped black
   walnuts or toasted English
   walnuts
Burnt Sugar Icing (page 64)
Garnish: ½ cup walnut halves

If you grew up in the Midwest, particularly Kansas, you would have especially fond memories of this rich, crunchy, moist cake, studded with black walnuts. If you don't live near a source of black walnuts, by all means substitute toasted English walnuts.

☆ ☆ ☆

Preheat the oven to 350° F. Lightly grease and flour a 9-inch by 13-inch pan. Set aside.

Sift together the flour, baking powder, and salt. Set aside.

In a large mixing bowl, beat the butter until creamy. Gradually add the sugars, beating until fluffy. Add the eggs, one at a time, beating well after each addition. Add the vanilla. Add the dry ingredients alternately with the milk, mixing just until the batter is smooth and blended. Fold in the nuts. Spoon the batter into the prepared pan.

Bake for 30 to 35 minutes, or until a cake tester inserted in the center of the cake comes out clean. Cool on a wire rack for about 10 minutes. Remove the cake from the pan and continue to cool. Frost with Burnt Sugar Icing when completely cool. Or cool and frost in the pan. Garnish with walnut halves.

YIELD: 12 TO 16 SERVINGS

Since 1955, Spencer, West Virginia, has been the site of an annual Black Walnut Festival in October. During the festival, some 13 tons of walnuts are hulled and consumed, as visitors watch parades, majorette competitions, gospel singers, black powder shoots, road races, antique car shows, and more. The highlight of the 4-day event is the black walnut bake-off competition.

For more information, contact the West Virginia Black Walnut Festival, P.O. Box 27, Spencer, West Virginia 25276 or phone 304-927-3340.

Poppy Seed Cake

☆☆☆☆☆☆☆☆☆☆☆☆☆☆☆☆☆☆☆☆

1 cup poppy seeds
1 cup milk
3 cups sifted cake flour
2½ teaspoons baking powder
½ teaspoon salt
1 cup butter or margarine
1¾ cups sugar
2 tablespoons cream sherry
2 teaspoons vanilla extract
6 egg whites, at room
   temperature
¼ teaspoon cream of tartar
¼ cup sugar
Garnish: Sifted confectioners
   sugar

C ookbooks are always exhorting the reader that fresh is better, but in the case of poppy seeds, it is especially true. Consider growing a patch of Oriental poppies and tasting the difference. The sight of the delicate flowers swaying in the wind is an additional bonus.

☆☆☆

Combine the poppy seeds and milk and let stand for several hours or overnight. Or, if pressed for time, combine the poppy seeds with warm milk and set aside for 1 hour.

Preheat the oven to 350° F. Lightly grease and flour a 10-inch tube or bundt pan or two 9-inch by 5-inch loaf pans. Set aside.

Sift together the flour, baking powder, and salt. Set aside.

In a large mixing bowl, beat the butter until creamy, then gradually add 1¾ cups sugar, beating until fluffy. Mix in the sherry and vanilla. Add the dry ingredients alternately with the poppy seed-milk mixture, mixing just until batter is smooth and blended.

In another bowl, beat the egg whites until foamy. Add the cream of tartar and beat until soft peaks form. Add the remaining ¼ cup of sugar gradually and beat until stiff but not dry. Stir one quarter of the egg whites into the batter, then gently fold in the remainder. Spoon the batter into the prepared pan(s).

Bake for 50 to 60 minutes in a tube or bundt pan, bake for 40 to 50 minutes in loaf pans, or until a cake tester inserted in the center of cake comes out clean. Cool on a wire rack for about 10 minutes. Remove the cake from the pan(s) and continue to cool. Sprinkle with confectioners sugar when completely cool.

YIELD: 10 TO 12 SERVINGS

But pleasures are
like poppies spread
You seize the flower,
its bloom is shed;
Or like the snow
falls in the river
A moment white,
then melts forever.

Robert Burns,
"Tam o' Shanter"

Angel Food Cake

☆ ☆ ☆ ☆ ☆ ☆ ☆ ☆ ☆ ☆ ☆ ☆ ☆ ☆ ☆ ☆ ☆

1¼ cups sifted cake flour
1½ cups sifted sugar
1¾ cups (about 12 to 14) egg
**   whites, at room**
**   temperature**
1¼ teaspoons cream of tartar
¼ teaspoon salt
1 teaspoon vanilla extract
½ teaspoon almond extract
Garnish: Sifted confectioners
**   sugar**

A great, billowy cloud of a cake, yes. But surely not invented by angels? More than one story is attached to the origins of this celestial dessert.

The most credible story is that it was invented by a frugal Pennsylvania Dutch cook who sought to use up egg whites left from the making of egg noodles. Another story credits an Indian cook who somehow sent the recipe to the States. The recipe wound up in the hands of a baker who baked the cakes behind shuttered windows to prevent competitors from stealing the recipe. At this time, the cake was also known as "mystery cake." Still another story sets down St. Louis as the location of the divine inspiration that led a certain Mr. Sides to make the cake with a secret recipe, which he sold for $25. The catch was that the cake could be made only with a secret white powder, which Mr. Sides also sold. The secret white powder was shortly revealed to be cream of tartar, which whitened the cake and made it tender, and soon the dish was seen on restaurant menus throughout St. Louis, a secret no longer.

☆ ☆ ☆

Preheat the oven to 300° F. Set out a 10-inch tube or angel cake pan. Do not grease.

Sift the flour with ½ cup of the sugar. Resift 3 more times. Set aside.

In the large bowl of an electric mixer, beat the egg whites until foamy. Add the cream of tartar and salt and beat until soft peaks form. Continue beating until stiff but not dry. Beat in the remaining 1 cup sugar, 1 tablespoon at a time, beating well after each addition until stiff peaks form. Beat in the vanilla and almond extracts.

Sift the flour and sugar mixture over the egg whites, about a quarter of it at a time. Using a rubber spatula or flat wire whisk, fold in the flour gently as you rotate the bowl. Continue folding in the flour by fourths until it is all incorporated.

Carefully spoon the batter into the ungreased pan. Pass a knife through batter, going around the pan twice to break up any air bubbles. Smooth the top.

Bake for 50 to 60 minutes, or until golden brown and the cake springs back when gently pressed. Remove from the oven. Invert the cake in the pan and let it cool upside down for 1 to 2 hours. If the pan doesn't have feet, you will have to rig something to enable the air to freely circulate under the cake. We recommend resting the tube opening on the neck of a glass beverage bottle or funnel.

When the cake is completely cool, run a thin spatula around the sides of the pan and center tube. Tap the bottom and sides of the pan to release the cake. Invert the cake and turn it out onto a platter. Sprinkle with confectioners sugar.

For a more elaborate presentation, horizontally slice the angel cake into 3 layers. Spread each layer with crushed sweetened strawberries or drained crushed pineapple. Cover with whipped cream—then coat the sides of the cake with whipped cream.

YIELD: 10 TO 12 SERVINGS

Sponge Cake

☆☆☆☆☆☆☆☆☆☆☆☆☆☆☆

1½ cups sifted cake flour
1½ teaspoons baking powder
½ teaspoon salt
½ cup (about 8) egg yolks
1¼ cups sugar
6 tablespoons boiling water
1 tablespoon lemon juice or
   1½ teaspoons vanilla
   extract
1 cup (about 8) egg whites, at
   room temperature
½ teaspoon cream of tartar
¼ cup sugar
Garnish: Sifted confectioners
   sugar

Few people regard sponge cake as an end to itself, but rather as the base for a luscious layering of cake, fruit, and cream. You can use sponge cake in trifles with custard and fruit, smother it under fresh summer berries, or marry it to ice cream. This cake is light, airy, and golden yellow.

☆ ☆ ☆

Preheat the oven to 325° F. Set out a 10-inch tube or angel food cake pan. Do not grease.

Sift together the flour, baking powder, and salt. Sift two more times, then leave the mixture in the sifter. Set aside.

In the large bowl of an electric mixer, beat the egg yolks until thick and lemon colored, about 5 minutes. Gradually add 1¼ cups of the sugar and beat an additional 5 minutes. Continue beating and add the boiling water in a steady stream. Beat until the mixture is light and fluffy. Add the lemon juice or vanilla.

Sift a third of the flour at a time over the egg yolk mixture. Using a rubber spatula, gently fold in the flour as you rotate the bowl. The folding in of the flour should take 2 to 3 minutes. Work carefully to avoid deflating the batter.

In another bowl, beat the egg whites until foamy. Add the cream of tartar and beat until soft peaks form. Continue beating until stiff but not dry. Beat in the remaining ¼ cup of sugar, 1 tablespoon at a time, beating well after each addition until stiff peaks form. Stir a quarter of the egg whites into the batter, then gently fold in the remainder, just until incorporated. Spoon the batter into the pan.

Bake for 50 to 55 minutes, or until a cake tester inserted in center of the cake comes out clean. Immediately invert the pan and let the cake cool upside down in the pan for about 2 hours. If the pan doesn't have feet, you will have to rig something to enable the air to freely circulate under the cake. We recommend resting the tube opening on the neck of a glass beverage bottle or funnel.

When the cake is completely cool, carefully cut away any crust that is stuck to the tube or rim of the pan. Run a thin spatula around the sides of the pan and center tube. Tap the bottom and sides of the pan to help release the cake. Invert the cake and turn it out onto a platter. Sprinkle with the confectioners sugar.

YIELD: 10 TO 12 SERVINGS

The baking is the most critical part of cake making. Test the oven with a piece of white paper. If it turns a light yellow in five minutes, it is ready for sponge cake; if a dark yellow in five minutes it is ready for cup cakes.

The All-Ways Preferable Cook Book, compiled by Miss Ada A. Hillier. Prepared for The Malleable Steel Range Mfg. Co., South Bend, Indiana (no date).

Pound Cake

☆ ☆ ☆ ☆ ☆ ☆ ☆ ☆ ☆ ☆ ☆ ☆ ☆ ☆

2 cups all-purpose
    unbleached flour
¼ teaspoon salt
1 cup butter, at room
    temperature
1¾ cups sugar
5 eggs, at room temperature
1½ teaspoons vanilla extract
    or 1 tablespoon lemon zest
    and 1 tablespoon lemon
    juice
Garnish: Sifted confectioners
    sugar

In the days before our heavy reliance on cookbooks, many cakes were reduced to easily remembered formulas. A one-two-three-four cake required 1 cup butter, 2 cups sugar, 3 cups flour, and 4 eggs. Likewise, the pound cake has an easily remembered formula: 1 pound of butter (2 cups), 1 pound of flour (4 cups), 1 pound of sugar (2 cups), and 1 pound of eggs (about 9). Those proportions make two 9-inch loaves or a single 10-inch tube pan. We don't follow those exact proportions anymore because our ingredients have changed. Butter has more fat and less water than it used to; flour, too, is less moist; and sugar is cleaner and therefore sweeter. This variation on the "half-pound" cake delivers good old-fashioned taste and a dense, velvety texture.

Preheat the oven 325° F. Lightly grease and flour a 9-inch by 5-inch loaf pan. Set aside.

Sift together the flour and salt. Set aside.

In the large bowl of an electric mixer, beat the butter until very light and creamy. Add the sugar gradually and continue beating for 5 minutes until mixture is very fluffy. Beat in the eggs, one at a time, beating well after each addition. Add the vanilla or lemon zest and juice. Fold in the dry ingredients, mixing just until the batter is smooth and blended. Spoon into the prepared pan.

Bake for 1¼ hours, or until a cake tester inserted in the center of the cake comes out clean. Cool on a rack for about 10 minutes. Remove the cake from the pan. Cool thoroughly and sprinkle with confectioners sugar.

YIELD: 12 SERVINGS

Beat with a knife
Will cause sorrow and strife;
Beat with a spoon
Will make heavy soon;
Beat with a fork
Will make light as a cork.

Anonymous. Reprinted in McCall's *Home Cook Book and General Guide*, compiled by Mrs. Jennie Harlan (New York: The McCall Company, 1890).

Honey Cake

☆☆☆☆☆☆☆☆☆☆☆☆☆☆☆

½ cup strong black coffee
1 cup dark honey
2½ cups sifted all-purpose
    unbleached flour
2 teaspoons baking powder
½ teaspoon baking soda
¼ teaspoon salt
1 teaspoon cinnamon
½ teaspoon ground ginger
½ teaspoon allspice
⅛ teaspoon ground cloves
3 eggs
¾ cup firmly packed dark
    brown sugar
⅓ cup vegetable oil
2 teaspoons orange zest
½ cup chopped walnuts
2 tablespoons candied finely
    shopped orange peel
    (optional)
Garnish: Sifted confectioners
    sugar

Honey cakes were standard fare at teas given by abolitionists in the early 1800s. They were popular because honey replaced the more common molasses, a sweetener produced by slave labor. Today, honey cake is a traditional dessert to serve on the Jewish New Year, where honey is eaten in hopes of having a sweet year. The rich honey cake goes well with raw apples dipped in honey, another New Year tradition.

☆ ☆ ☆

Preheat the oven to 300° F. Thoroughly grease and flour a 9-inch by 5-inch loaf pan. Set aside.

In a small saucepan, mix together the coffee and honey over moderate heat, stirring until combined. Set aside; cool to lukewarm.

Sift together the flour, baking powder, baking soda, salt, cinnamon, ginger, allspice, and cloves. Set aside.

In a mixing bowl, beat the eggs and brown sugar until light and fluffy. Gradually add the oil and continue beating until thoroughly blended. Add the orange zest. Add the dry ingredients alternately with the coffee/honey mixture, mixing just until the batter is smooth and blended. Fold in the nuts and candied orange peel. Spoon into the prepared pan.

Bake for 60 to 65 minutes, or until a cake tester inserted into the center of cake comes out clean. Cool on a wire rack for 10 minutes. Turn out of the pan and cool completely. Wrap in aluminum foil or plastic wrap and let stand overnight to allow the flavors to intensify. Sprinkle with confectioners sugar and cut into very thin slices.

YIELD: 12 SERVINGS

In the good old days, the housewife was not only responsible for making the cake, she had to take the honey from the hive as well. Here, then, is a procedure for removing honey from bee hives from McCall's Home Cook Book and General Guide, *compiled by Mrs. Jennie Harlan (New York: The McCall Company, 1890).*

Method of Taking Honey From Bee Hives Without Killing the Bees

Pour two teaspoonsful of chloroform into a piece of rag, double it twice, and place it on the floor-board of the hive, which must be lifted for the purpose, the entrance-hole being carefully secured. In about two minutes and a half there will be a loud humming, which will soon cease. Let the hive remain in this state for six or seven minutes, making about ten minutes in all. Remove the hive and the greater number of bees will be found lying senseless on the board; there will still be a few clinging to the combs, some of which may be brushed out with a feather. They return to animation in from half an hour to one hour after the operation. This plan possesses a great superiority over the usual mode of brimstoning, the bees being preserved alive; and over the more modern plan of fumigation by puff-ball; it is far less trouble, and the honey does not become tainted with the fumes.

Pineapple Upside Down Cake

☆ ☆

Topping

1 (20-ounce) can sliced
    pineapple
¼ cup butter or margarine
⅔ cup firmly packed dark
    brown sugar
16 pecan or walnut halves

Cake

1¼ cups sifted all-purpose
    unbleached flour
1½ teaspoons baking powder
¼ teaspoon ground ginger
¼ teaspoon salt
⅓ cup butter, margarine, or
    shortening, at room
    temperature
⅔ cup white sugar
1 egg
1 teaspoon vanilla extract
⅔ cup pineapple juice

Pineapple upside down cakes were first mentioned in cookbooks in the 1930s, though they were probably invented much earlier. Some books suggest that the pineapple upside down cake evolved from an earlier cake that was known as bachelor's bread. This was a sponge cake batter poured into a pan lined with thin slices of citron (which probably was a type of melon and not the rarely seen citrus fruit) and almonds. After the cake was baked, it was turned upside down onto a platter. The cake's name was a sly poke at the upside down nature of the bachelor's life—cooking being outside the normal range of male behavior at the time.

☆ ☆ ☆

Preheat the oven to 350° F.

To make the topping, drain the pineapple, reserving ⅔ cup of the juice. Over low heat, melt ¼ cup butter in a heavy 9-inch skillet. Or, if you are using a 9-inch Pyrex cake pan or pie plate, melt the butter in the oven. Sprinkle the brown sugar over the melted butter and spread the mixture evenly over the bottom of the pan. Remove from the heat. Arrange 8 pineapple slices over the brown sugar. Fill the centers and spaces between the pineapple with pecan halves placed flat side up.

Sift together the flour, baking powder, ginger, and salt. Set aside.

In a mixing bowl, beat the butter until creamy, then gradually add the sugar, beating until fluffy. Beat in the egg and vanilla. Add the dry ingredients alternately with the pineapple juice, mixing just until the batter is smooth and blended. Spoon the cake batter over the pineapple.

Bake for 40 to 45 minutes until done. Cool for 5 minutes. Loosen the cake around the edge. Invert onto a serving platter. Serve warm.

YIELD: 8 SERVINGS

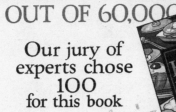

While pineapple canned in its own juice is an exceptionally fine canned fruit, fresh pineapple often has more texture and sharper flavor. To judge if a pineapple is ripe, look for bright green leaves. Try pulling out a leaf; if it yields easily, the fruit is ripe. The flesh should also feel slightly soft. The pineapple should have a distinctive pineapply smell.

Lemon Pudding Cake

☆☆☆☆☆☆☆☆☆☆☆☆☆☆☆☆☆☆☆☆☆☆☆☆

¾ cup sugar
¼ cup all-purpose unbleached
   flour
⅛ teaspoon salt
2 tablespoons melted butter
1 tablespoon lemon zest
5 tablespoons lemon juice
3 egg yolks
1½ cups milk
3 egg whites, at room
   temperature
⅛ teaspoon cream of tartar
¼ cup sugar

As the title suggests, this lovely, lemony dessert is a cross between a pudding and a cake. As it bakes it forms a creamy, custard bottom, topped by a spongy cake. To gild this lily, serve with cream, fresh berries, or a raspberry sauce made by pureeing a 10-ounce package of sweetened, frozen berries.

☆ ☆ ☆

Preheat the oven to 350° F. Lightly grease a 1½-quart baking dish or 6 custard cups. Set into a slightly larger pan, at least 2 inches deep.

In a mixing bowl, combine the ¾ cup sugar, flour, and salt. Add the butter, lemon zest, and lemon juice and mix until thoroughly blended.

With a whisk, beat the egg yolks until thick and lemon colored. Add the milk and mix well. Combine with the lemon mixture, stirring until blended.

In another bowl, beat the egg whites until foamy, add the cream of tartar, and beat until soft peaks form. Add the remaining ¼ cup of sugar gradually and beat until stiff but not dry. The egg whites should hold their shape and remain moist. Fold the whites into the lemon mixture. Spoon into the baking dish or custard cups. Pour 1 inch of hot water around them.

Bake until the pudding is set and the top is golden brown, about 35 minutes for the custard cups or 45 minutes for the baking dish. Remove the baking dish or custard cups from the water and let cool on a rack. Serve warm or chilled.

YIELD: 6 SERVINGS

Wonderful for Cake and Pastry as well as Bread

WASHBURN-CROSBY CO.

WASHBURN'S
TRADE MARK
Gold
MEDAL

FLOUR

WASHBURN - CROSBY CO.

GOLD MEDAL FLOUR

Doughnut Recipe

GOLD MEDAL FLOUR—2¾ cups	½ teaspoon salt
2 teaspoons baking powder	¾ cup milk
1 tablespoon shortening	1 egg
½ teaspoon nutmeg	½ cup sugar

Sift flour, baking powder, salt and nutmeg together. With two knives, cut the shortening. Add sugar and milk to well beaten egg and stir into the dry ingredients. Roll the dough out on a floured board, cut with doughnut cutter and fry in deep fat. The fat is the right temperature when it browns a crumb of bread in 60 seconds.

For other recipes write Washburn-Crosby Co.
Minneapolis, Minn.

We Sell and Recommend
GOLD MEDAL FLOUR
for all kinds of Baking

1905

Strawberry Shortcake

☆☆☆☆☆☆☆☆☆☆☆☆☆☆☆☆☆☆☆☆☆☆☆☆

Strawberries

6 cups fresh strawberries

3 tablespoons sugar, or to taste

1 tablespoon strawberry liqueur (framboise) or crème de cassis

Shortcake Biscuits

2 cups all-purpose unbleached flour

1 tablespoon baking powder

3 tablespoons sugar

½ teaspoon salt

½ cup chilled butter, cut into small pieces, or ¼ cup butter and ¼ cup solid vegetable shortening

⅔ cup milk or half-and-half

1 to 2 tablespoons soft butter

1 cup heavy whipping cream

2 tablespoons sifted confectioners sugar

⅛ teaspoon freshly grated nutmeg

There was a time, not so long ago, when strawberry season marked the beginning of summer, when fresh strawberries could be had from mid-June to mid-July only, and the idea of strawberries in February was unthinkable. And if you live in the north, the idea of strawberries in February is still unthinkable. The cello-packed berries shipped from who-knows-where are as tasteless as last summer's dried flowers. Strawberry shortcake, that quintessential summer dessert, can only be enjoyed when berries are fresh and local. And if there are pink stains on your hands from picking the strawberries yourself, and the berries are still warm from the sun, so much the better.

Set aside 6 strawberries for a garnish. Into a bowl, slice the remaining berries and sprinkle with 3 tablespoons of sugar and the strawberry liqueur. Toss until thoroughly combined. Cover and refrigerate for several hours, stirring occasionally.

Preheat the oven to 425° F. Lightly grease a cookie sheet.

To make the biscuits, sift together the flour, baking powder, sugar, and salt into a bowl. With a pastry blender or with your fingertips, cut or rub the butter into the dry ingredients until it has the consistency of coarse crumbs. Add the milk all at once, and stir with a fork until the dough just comes together.

Turn the dough out onto a lightly floured pastry cloth or board. Knead lightly about 12 to 15 times, sprinkling with a little flour if the dough is sticky. Roll out or pat the dough into a rectangle ½ inch thick. Cut into rounds with a floured 3-inch biscuit cutter or use a knife to cut into squares. Place the biscuits close together on the cookie sheet. The biscuits can be refrigerated for up to 2 hours before baking.

Bake for 15 to 18 minutes or until golden. Cool the biscuits briefly before removing them to a wire rack until cool enough to

handle. Split in half. Coat the bottom layer with a little soft butter. Whip the cream until stiff, add the confectioners sugar and nutmeg.

Transfer the bottoms of the shortcakes to individual serving plates and spoon some of the berries over each portion. Cover the berries with some of the whipped cream. Gently press on the top shortcake layer. Spoon the remaining strawberries over the top shortcake layer. Finish with another spoonful of whipped cream. Garnish each with a whole strawberry.

YIELD: 6 SERVINGS

If you are in Vermont in early June, and are near a field of Wild Strawberries, take half a day and pick enough for a Strawberry Shortcake. Until you have eaten shortcake made with the wild strawberries you have missed the treat of your life.

Gather and hull—don't attempt to wash—cover with sugar and let stand about an hour before putting on the shortcake which has been generously spread with butter. Now most folks would say "Don't spoil the flavor by putting cream on it," however, I'll leave that to you but at least try it with just the wild strawberries.

Many of the old cooks did not mash their berries, they cut them in halves about an hour before using them on the shortcake and covered them with sugar. Some cooks use whipped cream between the layers and on top, others use plain cream poured over the serving to suit the individual taste, still others never use any cream at all.

Many good old Vermont cooks consider it nothing less than heresy to use anything for the shortcake except baking powder biscuit, it might be all right to add an egg, but, in their estimation it's better plain and sponge or plain cake should never be used.

Wild red or black raspberries and blackberries also make delicious shortcake. The rules for preparation are the same as for strawberry shortcake.

From *A Vermont Cookbook by Vermont Cooks* (White River Junction, Vermont, 1958).

Praline Sour Cream Coffee Cake

☆☆☆☆☆☆☆☆☆☆☆☆☆☆☆☆☆☆☆☆☆☆☆☆☆☆☆☆☆☆

Cake

2 cups all-purpose unbleached
    flour
1½ teaspoons baking powder
½ teaspoon baking soda
¼ teaspoon salt
1 cup butter or margarine,
    at room temperature
2 cups sugar
2 teaspoons vanilla extract
2 eggs
1 cup sour cream

Streusel

2 tablespoons sugar
2 teaspoons cinnamon
1 cup chopped pecans

"My dear ladies:—To begin with, you must have nice rendered butter for baking purposes; I always buy enough butter in June to last all winter, for then it is cheap, say ten cents per pound, which is less than one-third what it is in winter, and it is not the 'fresh May butter' you get then either…" From *"Aunt Babette's" Cookbook. Foreign and Domestic. Receipts for the Household. A valuable collection of receipts and hints for the housewife, many of which are not to be found elsewhere* (Cincinnati and Chicago: The Bloch Publishing and Printing Co., 1891).

Preheat the oven to 350° F. Thoroughly grease and flour a 9-inch tube or bundt pan. Set aside.

Sift together the flour, baking powder, baking soda, and salt. Set aside.

In a mixing bowl, beat the butter until creamy, then gradually add the sugar and vanilla, beating until fluffy. Add the eggs, one at a time, beating well after each addition. Add the sour cream, mixing until smooth. Fold in the dry ingredients and beat just until blended. Do not overmix.

To make the streusel, combine the sugar, cinnamon, and pecans in a small bowl. Spoon half of the batter into the prepared pan. Sprinkle half of the streusel mixture evenly over the batter. Top with remaining batter and the rest of the streusel.

Bake for 55 to 60 minutes, or until a cake tester inserted in the center comes out clean. Cool the coffee cake on a rack for 20 minutes. Run a spatula carefully around the sides and center tube of pan before turning the cake out onto a rack. Serve warm.

YIELD: 10 TO 12 SERVINGS

During the nineteenth century, scripture cakes were popular. Half recipe, half puzzle, each ingredient was listed as a biblical verse, and the baker had to decipher its meaning. These recipes mostly exist in hand-written manuscripts, receipt books, handed down in families. This one was found in a book entitled A Vermont Cookbook by Vermont Cooks *(White River Junction, Vt., 1958).*

Scripture Cake

4 cups I Kings (first part)
1 cup Judges 5:25 (last clause)
2 cups Jeremiah 6:20
2 Cups I Samuel 30:12
2 cups Nahum 3:12 (found in the Apocrypha)
1 tablespoon Numbers 17:8
I large tablespoon I Samuel 14:25
Season to taste of II Chronicles 9:9
6 of Jeremiah 17:11
A pinch of Leviticus 2:13
½ cup Genesis 24:20
2 teaspoons Amos 4:5

Follow Solomon's advice for making good boys, Proverbs 23:14, and you will have a good cake.

Lindy's New York Cheesecake

☆☆☆☆☆☆☆☆☆☆☆☆☆☆☆☆☆☆☆☆☆☆☆☆☆☆☆☆☆☆

Cookie Dough Crust

1 cup all-purpose unbleached
   flour
3 tablespoons sugar
⅛ teaspoon salt
1 teaspoon lemon zest
½ cup butter or margarine, cut
   into ¼-inch cubes
1 egg yolk
½ teaspoon vanilla extract

Cheese Filling

2½ pounds cream cheese (five
   8-ounce packages), at room
   temperature
1¾ cups sugar
3 tablespoons all-purpose
   flour
2 teaspoons lemon zest
1 teaspoon lemon juice
1 teaspoon vanilla extract
5 eggs
2 egg yolks
¼ cup heavy cream

Cheesecakes are old, known to the ancient Greeks and popular over the centuries throughout Europe. The quintessential American cheesecake, a sweet, creamy, sinfully rich cake, was developed at Lindy's in New York, a restaurant known more for their clientele of celebrities than for their food. According to legend, waiters at Lindy's could be bribed to reveal the "secret" recipe. No doubt the bribery was widespread as this version is quite well known.

☆☆☆

First make the crust. Combine the flour, sugar, salt, and lemon zest in a large bowl. With a pastry blender or with your finger tips, cut or rub the butter into dry ingredients until it has the consistency of coarse crumbs. Add the egg yolk and vanilla. Mix until combined. Wrap in plastic and chill for 45 minutes.

Preheat the oven to 400° F. Pat the dough out over the bottom and 2 inches up the sides of a 9-inch springform pan. Bake for 10 minutes. Remove from the oven and set aside to cool. Reduce the oven temperature to 325° F.

To make the cheese filling, beat the batter by hand. If you use an electric mixer, avoid beating on very high speed because this incorporates too much air into the cheesecake and causes it to rise like a soufflé (and fall). Use a large mixing bowl and beat the cream cheese until it is creamy and smooth. Combine the sugar and flour and beat into the cream cheese. Add the lemon zest, lemon juice, and vanilla. Beat in the eggs and egg yolks, one at a time. Mix well after each addition. Beat in the cream, mixing until smooth. Pour the cheese mixture into the crust-lined pan and smooth the surface.

Bake for 1 to 1¼ hours, or until the center appears set. The cake will become firm as it chills. Remove from the oven and set in a draft-free place until it is completely cooled.

Gently run a sharp knife around the edge of pan. Refrigerate until thoroughly chilled.

Note: The original Lindy's recipe used a cookie dough crust, but if you prefer a crumb crust, prepare a graham cracker crust instead. Lightly grease a 9-inch springform pan. Preheat the oven to 325° F. Combine 1½ cups finely ground graham cracker crumbs, 3 tablespoons sugar, 6 tablespoons butter or margarine, melted, and ¼ teaspoon cinnamon. Press firmly into the bottom and 2 inches up the sides of the pan. Bake for 5 minutes. Set aside on a rack to cool.

YIELD: 8 TO 10 SERVINGS

Fudge Frosting

**4 ounces semi-sweet
  chocolate
¼ cup butter
4 cups confectioners sugar,
  sifted
⅛ teaspoon salt
½ cup milk
1 teaspoon vanilla extract**

This rich frosting hardens quickly, so be prepared to work fast. It is a good choice for both Devil's Food Cake (page 8) and Angel Food Cake (page 36).

☆ ☆ ☆

Combine the chocolate and butter and melt over very low heat, stirring constantly.

In a mixing bowl, combine the confectioners sugar, salt, milk, and vanilla. Beat until well combined. Add the butter mixture and beat until smooth. If the frosting is too thick, thin with a little more milk added a teaspoon at a time. If the frosting is too thin, allow it to stand for a few minutes, stirring occasionally. Once the frosting is the right consistency, work quickly as the frosting becomes hard on standing.

YIELD: FROSTING FOR THREE 8-INCH OR 9-INCH LAYERS
         OR A 9-INCH BY 13-INCH CAKE

*Come, butter, come
Come, butter, come;
Peter stands at the gate
Waiting for a butter cake,
Come, butter, come.*

This old English nursery rhyme made it across the Atlantic and was heard chanted by a butter maker as she churned as recently as 1936 in southern Indiana, according to the Oxford Dictionary of Nursery Rhymes *(1951). Marjorie Kinnan Rawlings reported a similar version of the rhyme in Florida in her book,* Cross Creek Cookery *(1942).*

Chocolate Frosting

☆☆☆☆☆☆☆☆☆☆☆☆☆☆☆☆☆☆☆☆

3 ounces unsweetened
   chocolate
3 tablespoons butter or
   margarine
3 cups sifted confectioners
   sugar
Pinch salt
7 tablespoons milk, at room
   temperature
1 teaspoon vanilla extract

A good all-purpose chocolate frosting, delicious with chocolate cakes (pages 8 to 12), Gold Cake (page 14), and Banana Cake (page 18). Try it on Carrot Cake (page 30) for a change from the usual cream cheese frosting.

☆ ☆ ☆

Combine the chocolate and butter and melt over very low heat, stirring until combined. Blend in the confectioners sugar and salt alternately with the milk and vanilla, mixing until the frosting is smooth and has a good consistency for spreading.

To give the frosting extra gloss and richness, add 1 egg yolk along with the milk. For extra flavor, substitute 1½ tablespoons of strong coffee, rum, or brandy for part of the milk.

YIELD: FROSTING FOR TWO 8-INCH OR 9-INCH LAYERS
          OR A 9-INCH BY 13-INCH CAKE

Glossy Chocolate Glaze

☆ ☆

1 cup (6 ounces) semi-sweet chocolate chips or chopped dark sweet baking chocolate
¼ cup butter
1 tablespoon light corn syrup

Excellent on the Chocolate Layer Cake (page 10), Gold Cake (page 14), Angel Food Cake (page 36), and Sponge Cake (page 38), this glaze hardens once it is spread on the cake and has a beautiful shine.

☆ ☆ ☆

In a heavy-bottomed saucepan, combine the chocolate, butter, and corn syrup. Cook over low heat, stirring until the mixture is melted and smooth. Cool for about 10 minutes, stirring occasionally. Then spread or pour over the cake.

YIELD: GLAZE FOR THE TOP AND SIDES OF AN 8-INCH
OR 9-INCH LAYER CAKE

Vanilla Frosting

☆☆☆☆☆☆☆☆☆☆☆☆☆☆☆☆☆☆

¼ cup butter or margarine, at
   room temperature
2 teaspoons lemon zest
3 cups sifted confectioners
   sugar
2 to 3 tablespoons cream or
   milk
1 teaspoon vanilla extract

This is a good frosting for Chocolate Layer Cake (page 10) and Banana Cake (page 18).

Beat the butter with the lemon zest until creamy. Gradually add half of the confectioners sugar, blending thoroughly. Beat in 2 tablespoons of the cream, the vanilla, and the remaining confectioners sugar. Add enough cream to make a smooth frosting of spreading consistency.

YIELD: FROSTING FOR TWO 8-INCH OR 9-INCH LAYERS
         OR A 9-INCH BY 13-INCH CAKE

With weights and measures just and true,
Oven of even heat,
Well buttered tins and quiet nerves
Success will be complete.

Anon. From *Cook Book by Royal Neighbors of America,* Baker Camp No. 2089, Peoria, Ill. (no date).

Seven Minute Frosting

☆ ☆

2 egg whites
1½ cups sugar
¼ teaspoon cream of tartar
⅓ cup water
Pinch salt
1 teaspoon vanilla extract

This is a fluffy, sweet frosting—good on Spice Cake (page 20) and Black Walnut Cake (page 32).

☆ ☆ ☆

In the top of a double boiler, combine the egg whites, sugar, cream of tartar, water, and salt. Place over simmering water (the water should not touch the bottom of the pan) and beat with an electric hand mixer or rotary beater for 7 minutes, or until stiff peaks form. Remove the pan from the boiling water, add the vanilla, and beat for another minute on high speed.

YIELD: FROSTING FOR TWO 8-INCH OR 9-INCH LAYERS
            OR A 9-INCH BY 13-INCH CAKE

Orange Frosting

☆ ☆ ☆ ☆ ☆ ☆ ☆ ☆ ☆ ☆ ☆ ☆ ☆ ☆ ☆ ☆ ☆

¼ cup butter or margarine, at
    room temperature
1 tablespoon orange zest
3 cups sifted confectioners
    sugar
About ¼ cup orange juice

We like this frosting on the Gold Cake (page 14) and Sponge Cake (page 38).

☆ ☆ ☆

To make the frosting, beat the butter with the orange zest until creamy. Gradually add half of the confectioners sugar, blending thoroughly. Beat in 2 tablespoons of the orange juice; then add the remaining confectioners sugar. Add enough orange juice to make a creamy frosting of spreading consistency.

YIELD: FROSTING FOR TWO 8-INCH OR 9-INCH LAYERS
             OR A 9-INCH BY 13-INCH CAKE

The Temperance Movement of the 1800s had its impact on cake baking, strange though that may sound. One arm of the movement, the religiously inspired Non-Fermentation Movement, wanted to ban the use of yeast in breads and cakes as yeast produces alcohol in the rising process, albeit in minute amounts. Instead, the use of baking powder, which produces a gas that raises the batter, was promoted. Some manufacturers of baking powder and other "safe, non-fermenting yeasts" also claimed to prevent rickets, cholera, and tooth decay while it promoted muscle and bone growth. The Non-Fermentation Movement got a boost when agents for Horsford's Self-Raising Bread Preparation distributed for free The Good Cook's Hand Book *in the 1860s and 1870s, which provided plenty of recipes using baking powder.*

Coconut Pecan Frosting

☆ ☆

3 egg yolks
1 cup evaporated milk
**¾ cup firmly packed light
  brown sugar**
½ cup butter or margarine
1 teaspoon vanilla extract
1 cup chopped pecans
**1¼ cups flaked sweetened
  coconut**

This frosting is traditional on the German Chocolate Cake (page 12). It is also wonderful on Spice Cake (page 20).

☆ ☆ ☆

In a heavy-bottomed saucepan, beat the egg yolks lightly with a wire whisk. Add the evaporated milk, brown sugar, and butter. Cook over low heat, stirring, until the mixture thickens, 8 to 10 minutes. Do not boil. Remove from the heat, add the vanilla, and cool, stirring frequently. Add the pecans and coconut and beat until the frosting is of spreading consistency.

YIELD: FROSTING FOR TWO 8-INCH OR 9-INCH LAYERS
        OR A 9-INCH BY 13-INCH CAKE

Sea Foam Frosting

☆☆☆☆☆☆☆☆☆☆☆☆☆☆☆☆☆☆☆☆☆

2 egg whites
1½ cups firmly packed light brown sugar
¼ teaspoon cream of tartar
⅓ cup of water
Pinch salt
1 teaspoon vanilla extract

A light frosting that contains no fat. It makes a lovely topping for Banana Cake (page 18), Spice Cake (page 20), and Black Walnut Cake (page 32).

In the top of a double boiler, combine the egg whites, brown sugar, cream of tartar, water, and salt. Place over simmering water (the water should not touch the bottom of the pan) and beat with an electric hand mixer or rotary beater for 7 minutes, or until the mixture forms stiff peaks. Remove the pan from the boiling water, add the vanilla, and beat for another minute on high speed, until the frosting is thick enough to spread.

YIELD: FROSTING FOR TWO 8-INCH OR 9-INCH LAYERS
OR A 9-INCH BY 13-INCH CAKE

Brown Sugar Frosting

☆ ☆ ☆ ☆ ☆ ☆ ☆ ☆ ☆ ☆ ☆ ☆ ☆ ☆ ☆ ☆ ☆ ☆ ☆ ☆

**1½ cups firmly packed dark
   brown sugar
1 tablespoon butter
5 tablespoons cream
Pinch salt
½ teaspoon vanilla extract**

The perfect topping for an Applesauce Cake (page 26) and
Poppy Seed Cake (page 34).

☆ ☆ ☆

In a small saucepan, combine the brown sugar, butter, cream, and
salt. Cook over medium heat, stirring constantly, until the mixture
comes to a boil. Remove from the heat. Cool slightly, then add the
vanilla and beat until the frosting is cool and slightly thickened. If
the frosting gets too thick, add a few drops of cream.

YIELD: FROSTING FOR A 9-INCH SQUARE OR TUBE CAKE

Cream Cheese Frosting

☆☆☆☆☆☆☆☆☆☆☆☆☆☆☆☆☆☆☆☆☆☆☆☆☆

½ cup butter or margarine, at
    room temperature
8 ounces cream cheese, at
    room temperature
2 teaspoons orange zest
2 cups sifted confectioners
    sugar

This is the classic frosting for Carrot Cake (page 30). It also works well on chocolate cakes (pages 8 and 12) and Spice Cake (page 20).

☆ ☆ ☆

In a bowl, beat the butter and cream cheese until creamy and well blended. Beat in the orange zest. Gradually add the confectioners sugar, beating until smooth.

YIELD: FROSTING FOR TWO 8-INCH OR 9-INCH LAYERS
        OR A 9-INCH BY 13-INCH CAKE

What To Do When You Don't Have the Right Size Pan

Of course, it is best to use the size pan specified in a recipe, but that isn't always possible. You may substitute another size pan, as long as the cake batter fills it at least 1 inch deep, otherwise the cake won't rise properly. For most cakes, fill the pans half to two-thirds full. Bundt, tube, and loaf pans may be filled a little higher. If you have too much batter, use the excess to fill muffin tins or custard cups.

Your baking time may need to be adjusted in a different size pan. Check for doneness by inserting a pick into the center of the cake. If it comes out clean, the cake is done. You can double-check by seeing that the cake pulls away from the sides of the pan and springs back when lightly pressed in the center.

Burnt Sugar Icing

☆☆☆☆☆☆☆☆☆☆☆☆☆☆☆☆☆☆☆☆☆☆☆

¼ cup sugar
⅓ cup boiling water
3 tablespoons butter or margarine, at room temperature
2¼ cups sifted confectioners sugar
1 teaspoon vanilla extract

We especially enjoy this on Black Walnut Cake (page 32). It is also very good on the Spice Cake (page 30) and the Pound Cake (page 40).

☆ ☆ ☆

Put the sugar in a small heavy saucepan or skillet and cook, without stirring, over medium heat until the sugar melts and the syrup becomes a deep golden brown. Remove from the heat. Slowly and carefully pour in the boiling water. (The water will steam and boil up as it hits the caramelized sugar.) Return the pan to a low heat and stir the mixture until the sugar is completely dissolved. Cool.

In a medium-size bowl, beat the butter until creamy. Gradually add half of the confectioners sugar, blending well. The mixture will be lumpy. Beat in 3 tablespoons of the cooled burnt sugar syrup and the vanilla. Blend in the remaining confectioners sugar and additional syrup to make a smooth frosting of spreading consistency.

YIELD: FROSTING FOR TWO 8-INCH OR 9-INCH LAYERS
OR A 9-INCH BY 13-INCH CAKE

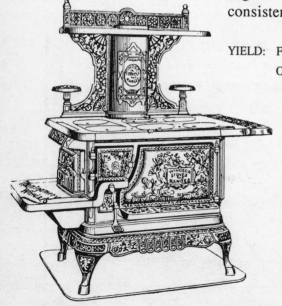

Frosting Tips

1. Start with a completely cooled cake. Brush off any crumbs and, if necessary, cut away any crisp edges.

2. Most frostings work best if made just before they are spread. Creamy, uncooked frostings can be held in the refrigerator for a few hours, if they are kept tightly covered. Warm to room temperature and stir well before using.

3. To keep the cake plate clean, place strips of waxed paper around the edges of the plate. These can be removed later.

4. Place the first layer, top side down on the cake plate. Spread with frosting almost to edge, using a frosting spatula.

5. Place the second layer, top side up, on the bottom layer.

6. Spread about three quarters of the remaining frosting on the sides. Hold the frosting spatula so that the tip rests on the cake plate. The straight edge of the blade should be held against the frosting so that the flat side of the blade forms a 30° angle with the side of the cake. Spread the frosting evenly on the sides. Don't worry about the ridge of frosting that piles up on the top of the cake. You will use that to cover the top.

7. With your spatula held horizontally and level, spread the remaining frosting on top of the cake, working from the edge to the center.

8. Use the back of a spoon to swirl circles and wavy lines in the frosting; pull up for peaks.

Pies

☆☆☆☆☆☆☆☆☆☆☆☆☆☆☆☆☆☆☆☆☆☆

Apple Pie

☆☆☆☆☆☆☆☆☆☆

Pastry for a 9-inch double crust (see page 110)
¾ **cup sugar or more to taste**
1½ **teaspoons cinnamon**
¼ **teaspoon nutmeg**
¼ **teaspoon allspice**
2 **tablespoons all-purpose unbleached flour**
3½ **to 4 pounds tart, crisp apples, peeled, cored, sliced ¼ inch thick (8 cups)**
1 **teaspoon lemon zest**
1 **tablespoon lemon juice**
2 **tablespoons butter or margarine, cut into small pieces**
1 **teaspoon milk**
1 **tablespoon sugar**

Apples and apple pie were both well known in the Old World. Indeed, there are indications that apples were known to the people of the Iron Age and were cultivated in Egypt some 4,000 years ago. The Pilgrims brought with them apple seeds and lost no time in getting trees established. Apple orchards were so valuable that by 1648 Governor John Endicott was able to trade 500 apple trees for 250 acres of land. By the end of the 19th century, some 8,000 apple varieties were listed with the USDA. Is it any wonder that apple pie became one of America's most popular desserts?

☆ ☆ ☆

Prepare the pie dough according to the recipe directions and refrigerate.

In a large bowl, combine ¾ cup sugar, the cinnamon, nutmeg, allspice, and flour. Add the apples; sprinkle with lemon zest and lemon juice. Toss together to thoroughly mix. If the apples are too tart, add a little extra sugar.

Preheat the oven to 425° F.

To prepare the crust, roll out the larger portion of the chilled dough and line a 9-inch pie plate, leaving a 1-inch overhang. Spoon the apple mixture into the pastry, mounding it higher in the center. Dot with butter. Roll out the remaining dough into a circle about 1 inch larger than the pie plate. Moisten the edge of the bottom crust with water. Fold the dough circle in half, lift off the board, place it across the center of the filled pie, and unfold. Trim the edge ½ inch larger than pie plate and tuck the overhang under the edge of bottom crust. Crimp the edges together with a fork or make a fluted pattern with your fingers. Make several decorative slits into the top crust to allow steam to escape.

Place the pie on a baking sheet to catch any juices that overflow. Bake in the lower third of oven for 45 to 50 minutes.

About 10 minutes before the pie is done, brush the top with milk and sprinkle with the remaining 1 tablespoon of sugar.

Cool the pie on a rack. Serve warm or at room temperature with slices of cheddar cheese or vanilla ice cream.

YIELD: 6 TO 8 SERVINGS

The friendly cow all red and white,
I love with all my heart:
She gives me cream with all her might,
To eat with apple tart.

Robert Louis Stevenson, "The Cow"

But I, when I undress me
Each night, upon my knees
Will ask the Lord to bless me
With apple-pie and cheese.

Eugene Field, "Apple-Pie and Cheese"

Gail Borden

What he and his successors did for you

Milk is the most necessary single article of food in the world, but milk is more susceptible to contamination than almost any other food. It is essential that milk should be plentiful and accessible, but it is equally essential that it should be pure.

The man who first realized these facts and then invented the processes which made it possible for the entire world to have pure milk at any time, in any quantity and under all conditions, was Gail Borden. He invented condensed milk, he introduced the system which takes care of the milk from the cow to your cup in its pristine purity, a system preceding strict governmental regulations but found in accord with them when introduced.

Gail Borden left behind him an organization that has grown to be the largest in the world for the handling of milk, an organization inspired by his zeal, his honesty and his ability, an organization which has made his name a synonym for milk—fresh—condensed—evaporated—cultured—malted—every form of milk, but always pure and always good.

Borden's Fluid Milk is delivered fresh on the two largest milk routes in the world, one centering in New York, and one in Chicago

MILK

Borden's Eagle Brand Condensed Milk has successfully fed and raised more infants than any one single prepared infants' food in the world

BORDEN'S CONDENSED MILK COMPANY
NEW YORK, U. S. A.

Blueberry Pie

☆☆☆☆☆☆☆☆☆☆☆☆☆☆☆☆☆

Pastry for a 9-inch double
crust pie (see page 110)
6 cups fresh blueberries
¾ cup sugar
5 tablespoons all-purpose
unbleached flour
Pinch salt
1 teaspoon cinnamon
¼ teaspoon nutmeg
1 tablespoon lemon juice
1 tablespoon butter or
margarine, cut into pieces
1 egg, beaten
1 tablespoon water

E at in any diner in New England in summer and you are likely to find blueberry pie on the menu. If you are lucky, the pie will be filled with fresh berries. Unlucky travelers will be served a sweet, blue, gluey concoction that goes by the name of blueberry pie. In that case, it's best to bake your own.

☆ ☆ ☆

Prepare the pie dough according to the recipe directions and refrigerate. Rinse and sort the blueberries. Drain thoroughly on paper towels.

In a large bowl, combine the sugar, flour, salt, cinnamon, and nutmeg. Add the blueberries, sprinkle with lemon juice. Toss lightly to combine. Set aside.

Preheat the oven to 425° F.

To prepare the pie shell, roll out the larger portion of the chilled dough and line a 9-inch pie plate, leaving a 1-inch overhang. Spoon the filling into the pastry. Dot with butter. Roll out the remaining dough into a circle about 1 inch larger than the pie plate. Moisten the edge of the bottom crust with water. Fold the dough circle in half, lift off the board, place it across the center of filled pie, and unfold. Trim the edge ½ inch larger than the pie plate and tuck the overhang under the edge of bottom crust. Crimp the edges together with a fork or make a fluted pattern with your fingers. Make several decorative slits into the top crust to allow steam to escape.

Make an egg wash by combining the egg with the water. Brush the top of the pie with the egg wash. Place the pie on a baking sheet to catch any juices that overflow.

Bake in the lower third of the oven for 15 minutes. Reduce the oven temperature to 350° F. and bake for 40 to 45 minutes or until the crust is golden brown. Cool the pie on a rack. Serve warm or at room temperature.

YIELD: 6 TO 8 SERVINGS

*The annual State of Maine Blueberry Festival is held
during the last week in August in Union, Maine.
Here's your chance to eat free blueberry pies, which
are baked on the fairgrounds and served to everyone
who stops in at the Blueberry Hut each afternoon.
You can begin each day with blueberry pancakes,
meet the reigning blueberry princess, and spend your
mornings sampling fresh blueberries, blueberry jam,
and blueberry syrup. Don't forget the blueberry pie
eating contest.*

For more information, contact the Maine
Blueberry Festival: 207-785-4173.

Lattice-Top Sour Cherry Pie

☆☆☆☆☆☆☆☆☆☆☆☆☆☆☆☆☆☆☆☆☆☆☆☆☆☆☆☆☆

Pastry for a 9-inch double crust pie (see page 110)
2 (16-ounce) cans water-packed pitted sour cherries or 6 to 7 cups pitted fresh sour cherries
¾ cup sugar
3 tablespoons cornstarch
Pinch salt
⅛ teaspoon ground cloves
1 teaspoon lemon juice
¼ teaspoon almond extract
1 tablespoon butter or margarine, cut into small pieces
1 teaspoon milk
1 tablespoon sugar

I t takes a dedicated baker to make a sour cherry pie from scratch. First you must stake out your tree and harvest the fruit before the birds get them. Then you must pit the cherries, a process that is laborious and unrewarding (there's no pleasure in popping an occasional cherry into your mouth). A gadget exists for stoning cherries, but a paper clip works just as well.

If this kind of labor isn't fun, rely on canned cherries.

Prepare the pie dough according to the recipe directions and refrigerate.

If you are using canned cherries, drain the cherries and reserve ⅓ cup of the juice. If you are using fresh cherries, combine the cherries with 3 tablespoons of water in a large saucepan. Heat to boiling, stirring gently for 1 minute. Remove from the heat, drain off the juice to measure ⅓ cup. If there isn't enough liquid, add more water. Cool completely.

In a heavy saucepan, combine the sugar, cornstarch, and salt. Add the cherry juice and stir with a whisk until blended. Place over medium heat, stirring until the sugar is dissolved. Boil for 2 to 3 minutes, stirring constantly until the mixture is slightly thickened. Remove from heat; stir in the cloves, lemon juice, and almond extract. Carefully mix in cherries. Set aside to cool.

Preheat the oven to 425° F.

To prepare the pie shell, roll out the larger portion of the chilled dough and line a 9-inch pie plate, leaving a 1-inch overhang. Spoon the cooled filling into pastry. Dot with butter. Roll out the remaining dough into a rectangle about ⅛ inch thick and 11 inches long. Trim the ragged edges. Using a pastry wheel or sharp knife, cut the rectangle into 10 lengthwise strips, each ½ inch wide. To form the lattice, lay 5 strips across the filling 1 inch apart. Working from the center, interweave the remaining strips, one at a time, over and under the first strips. Trim the ends. Moisten the overhanging edge of the bottom crust and fold up over ends of the strips. Flute the edge of the crust. Brush the lattice strips with milk; sprinkle with the remaining tablespoon of sugar.

Place the pie on a baking sheet to catch any juices that overflow. Bake in the lower third of the oven for 15 minutes. Reduce the oven temperature to 350° F. and bake for an additional 30 minutes, or until bubbly and golden brown. Cool the pie on a wire rack. Serve warm or at room temperature.

YIELD: 6 TO 8 SERVINGS

Who dares deny the truth,
There's poetry in pie?

Henry Wadsworth Longfellow

Strawberry Rhubarb Pie

☆ ☆

Pastry for a 9-inch double crust pie (see page 110)
1¼ cups sugar
⅓ cup all-purpose unbleached flour
Pinch salt
1 teaspoon orange zest
1 pound fresh rhubarb, cut into 1-inch pieces (4 cups)
2 cups halved strawberries
2 tablespoons butter or margarine
1 teaspoon milk
1 tablespoon sugar

Pie plant, as rhubarb is also known, is a native to Asia and Eastern Europe, where it is valued both for medicinal properties and for eating. You can't do much with rhubarb but cook it with plenty of sugar or honey to make a sauce or a pie. Conveniently, the tart rhubarb matures just as sweet strawberries ripen, allowing for a marriage that was surely arranged in heaven.

Prepare the pie dough according to the recipe directions and refrigerate. In a large bowl, combine the sugar, flour, salt, and orange zest. Add the rhubarb and strawberries and toss lightly to combine. Set aside.

Preheat the oven to 425° F.

To prepare the pie shell, roll out the larger portion of the chilled dough and line a 9-inch pie plate, leaving a 1-inch overhang. Spoon the filling into the pastry. Dot with butter. Roll out the remaining dough into a rectangle about ⅛ inch thick and 11 inches long. Trim the ragged edges. Using a pastry wheel or sharp knife, cut the rectangle into 10 lengthwise strips, each ½ inch wide. To form the lattice, lay 5 strips across the filling 1 inch apart. Working from the center, interweave the remaining strips, one at a time, over and under the first strips. Trim the ends. Moisten the overhanging edge of the bottom crust and fold up over the ends of the strips. Flute the edge of the crust. Brush the lattice strips with milk; sprinkle with a tablespoon of sugar. Place the pie on a baking sheet to catch any juices that overflow.

Bake in the lower third of the oven for 15 minutes. Reduce the oven temperature to 350° F. and bake for an additional 50 minutes, or until bubbly and golden brown. Cool the pie on a wire rack. Serve warm or at room temperature with whipped cream or vanilla yogurt.

YIELD: 6 TO 8 SERVINGS

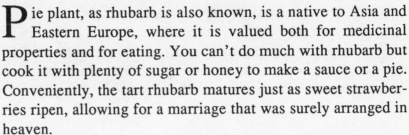

Little Girl's Pie

Take a deep dish, the size of a soup plate, fill it, heaping, with peeled tart apples, cored and quartered; pour over it one tea-cup of molasses, and three great spoonfuls of sugar, dredge over this a considerable quantity of flour, enough to thicken the syrup a great deal. Cover it with a crust made of cream, if you have it, if not, common dough, with butter worked in, or plain pie crust, and lap the edge over the dish, and pinch it down tight, to keep the syrup from running out. Bake about an hour and a half. Make several at once, as they keep well.

Miss Beecher's Domestic Receipt-Book by Catherine Esther Beecher (sister of author Harriet Beecher Stowe) (New York: Harper and Bros., 1868).

Deep-Dish Peach Pie

☆☆☆☆☆☆☆☆☆☆☆☆☆☆☆☆☆☆☆☆☆☆☆☆☆☆

**Cream Cheese Pastry
   (page 114)**
**6 cups fresh peeled, sliced
   peaches**
**3 tablespoons all-purpose
   unbleached flour**
**¼ cup firmly packed light
   brown sugar, or to taste**
**⅛ teaspoon freshly grated
   nutmeg**
**2 tablespoons butter, cut into
   small pieces**
1 egg yolk
2 teaspoons water
1 teaspoon white sugar

O ne has to live in peach country—the Southeast, New Jersey, and the Pacific Northwest—to enjoy a perfect tree-ripened peach these days. For the rest of us, peaches bought a few days in advance and left to ripen in a paper bag with a banana or an apple will do.

Prepare the pastry dough according to the recipe directions and refrigerate.

Preheat the oven to 375° F. Place the peaches in an 8-inch square baking dish or 2-quart casserole.

In a small bowl, combine the flour, brown sugar, and nutmeg. Toss with the peaches, mixing gently until they are thoroughly coated. Dot with butter.

On a lightly floured pastry cloth or board, roll out the pastry into a square or circle 1 inch larger than the baking dish. Roll the pastry onto the rolling pin and then gently drape it over the top of the dish. Crimp the edges of the pastry and press around the top of the dish. Brush the surface with an egg wash made by beating the egg yolk with the water. Sprinkle with the white sugar. With the tip of a sharp knife cut 3 to 4 slits in top of pastry to allow steam to escape.

Bake for 35 to 40 minutes or until the crust is golden. Serve warm along with a scoop of vanilla ice cream or a spoonful of heavy cream.

YIELD: 6 SERVINGS

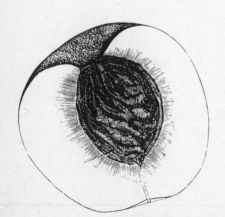

The peach has made a very successful journey from China to the New World. Actually, it went from China to Persia to Rome and then throughout Europe. The fruit bore the name Persian apple, which in Middle English became peche. *The Spanish brought the peach to the New World in the 17th century.*

Sour Cream Raisin Pie

☆☆☆☆☆☆☆☆☆☆☆☆☆☆☆☆☆☆☆☆☆☆☆☆☆☆☆

Partially baked 8-inch pie
   shell (see page 110)
2 eggs
¾ cup sugar
1 cup sour cream
½ teaspoon cinnamon
¼ teaspoon nutmeg
Pinch salt
1 cup chopped raisins
Zest of 1 lemon
1 tablespoon lemon juice
½ cup chopped walnuts

We've eaten many different versions of raisin pie in our days. Raisin pies made in Vermont are likely to be sweetened with maple syrup. Some pies are made without sour cream, in which case, they bear a striking resemblance to mince pies. This version has a custard base and is delicately spiced.

☆ ☆ ☆

Prepare the pie shell according to the recipe directions. Partially bake and let cool on a rack before filling.

Preheat the oven to 425° F.

In a bowl, beat the eggs and sugar with a wire whisk until light and fluffy. Add the sour cream, cinnamon, nutmeg, salt, raisins, lemon zest, and lemon juice, mixing until well blended. Pour the mixture into the pie shell. Sprinkle the walnuts over the top.

Bake in the lower third of the oven for 10 minutes, reduce the oven temperature to 350° F., and continue baking for 25 to 30 minutes, or until a knife inserted 1 inch from the edge comes out clean. (If the rim of the crust browns too quickly, cover the edge with a strip of aluminum foil.) Cool the pie on a rack. Serve at room temperature or chilled. Refrigerate any leftover pie.

YIELD: 6 SERVINGS

The summer of 1873 was a hot one, so hot that in California grapes were drying on the vine. It was a financial disaster for the growers—except for one who shipped his dried grapes to a friend in San Francisco who ran a grocery store. The grocer, an enterprising fellow, called the grapes "Peruvian delicacies" simply because there was a Peruvian ship in the harbor at the time and he had no better name for them. The raisins were a sweet success, and grape growing in the San Joaquin Valley was never the same.

Pumpkin Pie

☆ ☆ ☆ ☆ ☆ ☆ ☆ ☆ ☆ ☆ ☆ ☆ ☆ ☆

**Unbaked 9-inch pie shell
(see page 110)
2 eggs
¾ cup firmly packed light
brown sugar
2 cups cooked or canned
pureed pumpkin
1 teaspoon cinnamon
1 teaspoon ground ginger
½ teaspoon nutmeg
¼ teaspoon ground cloves
¼ teaspoon allspice
½ teaspoon salt
1½ cups (12-ounce can)
evaporated milk
2 tablespoons orange liqueur
(Grand Marnier)**

I f you love pumpkin pie, chances are you won't want to miss the opportunity to eat from the world's largest pumpkin pie— a phenomenon that weighs in at 350 pounds and measures 5 feet in diameter. It all happens at the Circleville Pumpkin Show, which has been held in October in Circleville, Ohio, for over 80 years. Each year some 400,000 visitors spend 4 days eating pumpkin pie, doughnuts, fudge, pancakes, bread, cake, and ice cream. For entertainment there are displays of pumpkin crafts, pumpkins of unusual shapes, pie eating contests, and, even, the Miss Pumpkin Beauty Show. The organizers call it the "Greatest Free Show on Earth." (For information on this year's show, contact the Circleville Chamber of Commerce, 135 West Main Street, P.O. Box 462, Circleville, Ohio 43113; or call 614-474-4923.)

☆ ☆ ☆

Prepare the pie shell according to the recipe directions and refrigerate.

Preheat the oven to 425° F.

In a bowl, beat together the eggs and sugar until light. Mix in the pumpkin, cinnamon, ginger, nutmeg, cloves, allspice, salt, evaporated milk, and orange liqueur and blend thoroughly. Pour into the unbaked pie shell.

Bake in the lower third of the oven for 15 minutes, reduce the oven temperature to 325° F., and continue baking for 35 to 40 minutes, or until the filling is firm and a knife inserted 1 inch from the edge comes out clean.

Cool on a rack. Serve at room temperature or chilled with whipped cream or Ginger Spiced Whipped Cream. Refrigerate any leftover pie.

Ginger Spiced Whipped Cream

Beat 1 cup heavy whipping cream until soft peaks form. Add 1 tablespoon brandy and 2 tablespoons sifted confectioners sugar and beat until stiff. Fold in 2 tablespoons sour cream and 2 tablespoons minced crystallized ginger.

YIELD: 6 TO 8 SERVINGS

The Pilgrims enjoyed a no-fuss pumpkin dessert. They removed the top of the pumpkin, scooped out the fibers and seeds, and baked the shell. When the pulp was done, milk flavored with spices and honey was poured in, and the resulting pudding was eaten right out of the pumpkin.

Sweet Potato Pie

☆ ☆ ☆ ☆ ☆ ☆ ☆ ☆ ☆ ☆ ☆ ☆ ☆ ☆ ☆ ☆ ☆ ☆

Unbaked 9-inch pie shell
   crust (see page 000)
2 eggs
¾ cup firmly packed dark
   brown sugar
2 cups mashed, cooked
   sweet potatoes
1 tablespoon all-purpose
   unbleached flour
1½ teaspoons cinnamon
½ teaspoon ground ginger
½ teaspoon nutmeg
¼ teaspoon allspice or mace
¼ teaspoon ground cloves
½ teaspoon salt
3 tablespoons butter, melted
   and cooled
1½ cups half-and-half or
   evaporated milk
1 tablespoon bourbon or
   brandy

Thought to originate in South America, the sweet potato was cultivated in North America long before Columbus set off from Spain. In the South, sweet potato pies are much more common than pumpkin pies.

Prepare the pie shell according to the recipe directions andrefrigerate.

Preheat the oven to 425° F.

In a bowl, beat together the eggs and sugar until light. Mix in the sweet potatoes, flour, cinnamon, ginger, nutmeg, allspice, cloves, salt, butter, half-and-half, and bourbon and blend thoroughly. Pour the mixture into the unbaked pie shell.

Bake in the lower third of the oven for 15 minutes, then reduce the oven temperature to 325° and continue baking for 35 to 40 minutes, or until the filling is firm and a knife inserted 1 inch from the edge comes out almost clean. (A little sweet potato will adhere to the knife.)

Cool on a rack. Serve at room temperature or chilled, with whipped cream sweetened with honey and sprinkled with freshly grated nutmeg. Refrigerate any leftover pie.

YIELD: 6 TO 8 SERVINGS

What moistens the lip
And what brightens the eye;
What calls back the past,
Like rich pumpkin pie?

John Greenleaf Whittier, "The Pumpkin"

Pecan Pie

☆ ☆ ☆ ☆ ☆ ☆ ☆ ☆ ☆ ☆ ☆

Partially baked 9-inch pie
  shell (see page 110)
2 tablespoons butter or
  margarine, at room
  temperature
¾ cup firmly packed dark
  brown sugar
2 tablespoons all-purpose
  unbleached flour
¼ teaspoon salt
1 cup light corn syrup
3 eggs
1 teaspoon vanilla extract
1 tablespoon dark rum
1¼ cups toasted pecan
  halves

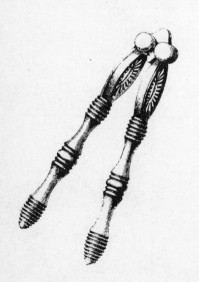

"As American as Pecan Pie" should be the saying. Pecans, like corn and cranberries, are native to North America and were introduced to the early colonists by the native Americans. The name is derived from an Indian word meaning "hard-shelled nut."

Thomas Jefferson is often credited with the spread of the pecan's popularity. He planted hundreds of trees at Monticello and gave seedlings to George Washington, who planted them at Mount Vernon, where there are still pecan trees today—most likely descendants of the original planting.

☆ ☆ ☆

Prepare the pie shell according to the recipe directions. Partially bake and cool on a rack before filling.

Preheat the oven to 350° F.

In a bowl, beat the butter until creamy. Add the brown sugar, flour, and salt and mix together until thoroughly combined. Blend in the corn syrup. Add the eggs, one at a time, beating well after each addition. Add the vanilla and rum.

Spread the pecans over the pie crust. Pour the egg mixture over the pecans. Bake for 35 to 40 minutes or until the filling is firm.

Cool the pie on a wire rack. Serve warm or at room temperature with whipped cream flavored with rum or vanilla ice cream.

Note: To toast pecans, preheat the oven to 300° F. Place the pecans on a baking sheet and bake for 6 to 8 minutes, stirring once. Cool.

YIELD: 6 TO 8 SERVINGS

For pottage and puddings, and custards, and pies,
Our pumpkins and parsnips are common supplies.
We have pumpkins at morning and pumpkins at noon;
If it were not for pumpkins, we should be undoon.

Anonymous (c. 1630)

Shoofly Pie

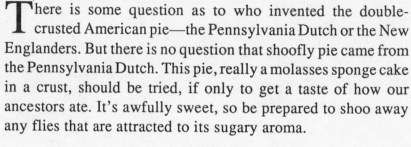

Unbaked 9-inch pie shell
(see page 110)
1¼ cups all-purpose
unbleached flour
½ cup firmly packed light
brown sugar
½ teaspoon cinnamon
¼ teaspoon nutmeg
¼ teaspoon salt
¼ cup butter or margarine,
at room temperature
½ teaspoon baking soda
⅔ cup hot water
⅔ cup dark molasses

There is some question as to who invented the double-crusted American pie—the Pennsylvania Dutch or the New Englanders. But there is no question that shoofly pie came from the Pennsylvania Dutch. This pie, really a molasses sponge cake in a crust, should be tried, if only to get a taste of how our ancestors ate. It's awfully sweet, so be prepared to shoo away any flies that are attracted to its sugary aroma.

Prepare the pie shell according to the recipe directions and refrigerate. Preheat the oven to 425° F.

In a bowl, combine the flour, brown sugar, cinnamon, nutmeg, and salt. Using your fingers, rub the butter into the dry ingredients until the mixture has the consistency of coarse meal.

Dissolve the baking soda in the hot water; combine with the molasses. Pour one third of the molasses mixture into the bottom of the unbaked pie shell. Sprinkle with one third of the crumb mixture. Continue layering, ending with the crumb mixture.

Bake in the lower third of the oven for 15 minutes, reduce the oven temperature to 350° F., and continue baking for 20 minutes, or until the filling is firm when lightly pressed with your fingertip.

Let cool on a wire rack. Serve warm or cold with light cream.

YIELD: 6 TO 8 SERVINGS

To make a light, crisp, and flaky crust, use a good, fine flour and none but the best butter. Have everything, including yourself, cool. A marble slab makes the best pastry-board. Use a glass rolling-pin, if convenient; if not, one made from hard wood with movable handles. Always use ice or very cold water in mixing, and keep the paste in a cold place. . . . No matter how light your paste may be, the substance of each stratum is dense and hard of digestion, and should never be eaten by persons of weak digestive powers.

Mrs. Rorer's Cook Book, A Manual of Home Economics
by Mrs. S. T. Rorer (Philadephia: Arnold and Company, 1866).

Chess Pie

☆ ☆ ☆ ☆ ☆ ☆ ☆ ☆ ☆ ☆ ☆

**Partially baked 9-inch pie
  shell (see page 110)**
**⅓ cup butter or margarine, at
  room temperature**
½ cup white sugar
**½ cup firmly packed brown
  sugar**
3 eggs
**1 tablespoon all-purpose
  unbleached flour**
**1 tablespoon yellow
  cornmeal**
⅛ teaspoon salt
¼ cup heavy cream
1½ teaspoons vanilla extract
1 cup chopped pecans

How did this southern specialty get its name? A few stories circulate, none of which have anything to do with the ancient board game. Some claim that a chess pie was originally a "chest pie," or the kind of pie that would keep in a chest or cupboard without refrigeration. Some say that it is an adaptation of the English cheese pie. Then there is the story of the plantation cook who was asked what she was making. "Jes' pie," she replied.

Whatever the origin, today there are many variations. This version is similar to the Thomas Jefferson version. Another version, which contains spices and dates, is called a Jefferson Davis Pie.

☆ ☆ ☆

Prepare the pie shell according to the recipe directions. Partially bake and let cool on a rack before filling. Preheat the oven to 350° F.

In a large mixing bowl, beat together the butter and sugars until creamy. Add the eggs, one at a time, beating well after each addition. Stir in the flour, cornmeal, salt, cream, vanilla, and pecans, blending well. Pour the mixture into the pie shell. Bake for 40 to 45 minutes, or until a knife inserted 1 inch from the outer edge comes out clean, and the filling is slightly firm.

Cool on a wire rack. Serve warm or at room temperature. This pie tastes best when it is eaten within 3 hours of cooling. Refrigerate any leftover pie.

YIELD: 6 TO 8 SERVINGS

GRAND OPERA HOUSE COMMENCING **MONDAY, DEC. 4**
Saturday Matinees Only.

Lotta.

By a certain definition, a Yankee is one who eats pie for breakfast. But the great pie makers were probably from Dixie. According to food historians, pie making became something of a mania in the South in the 19th century. This coincided with the drop in the price of white sugar as the cane sugar industry developed in the States. No more did cooks have to depend on strongly flavored honey and sorghum to sweetened their pastries. Instead, they could whip up such blandly sweet delights as Chess Pie and Pecan Pie and Lemon Meringue.

Coconut Custard Pie

☆☆☆☆☆☆☆☆☆☆☆☆☆☆☆☆☆☆☆☆☆☆

**Partially baked 9-inch pie
   shell (see page 110)**
**1 cup sweetened flaked
   coconut**
4 eggs
⅔ cup sugar
¼ teaspoon salt
⅛ teaspoon nutmeg
1½ teaspoons vanilla extract
**2½ cups hot (not boiling)
   milk or half-and-half**
**1 tablespoon Apricot Glaze
   (see page 118)**
**Garnish: Freshly grated
   nutmeg**

As anyone who has eaten this pie in a diner can attest, it is prone to a soggy crust. Eat this within a few hours of baking, and no one will have any complaints.

☆ ☆ ☆

Prepare the pie shell according to the recipe directions. Partially bake and let cool on a rack before filling.

Preheat the oven to 300° F. and toast the coconut on a cookie sheet for about 10 minutes, stirring frequently, until golden brown. Watch carefully to see that the coconut doesn't burn. Remove from the pan and set aside. Increase the oven temperature to 425° F.

In a bowl, beat the eggs slightly with a whisk. Stir in the sugar, salt, nutmeg, and vanilla. Add the hot milk gradually, stirring constantly. Set aside.

Brush the pie shell with the apricot glaze, then sprinkle the coconut over the glaze. Place the unfilled pie shell on a shelf in the lower third of the oven. Carefully pour or ladle the custard filling into the shell.

Bake for 15 minutes, reduce the oven temperature to 350° F. and bake for 20 minutes longer, or until a knife inserted 1 inch from the outer edge comes out clean. The center may look a little bit soft but will firm up later. Remove from the oven and sprinkle the top with nutmeg.

Cool on a wire rack. Serve warm or at room temperature. Custard pies are best if eaten within 3 hours of cooling. Refrigerate any leftover pie, but expect that the pie shell will get soggy in the refrigerator.

YIELD: 6 TO 8 SERVINGS

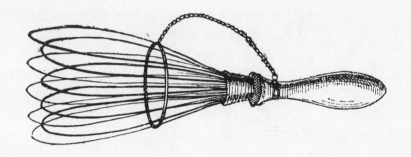

Whisks were invaluable for beating egg whites, cream, and batters in the days before electric mixers. But in colonial times, one wouldn't necessarily find a whisk among the various sundries sold door-to-door by the Yankee peddler. A book-learned cook, however, could find instructions for making a whisk in a book entitled, A Perfect School of Instructions For the Officers of the Mouth; shewing The Whole Art of A Master of the Household, A Master Carver, A Master Butler, A Master Confectioner, A Master Cook, A Master Pastryman Being a Work of Singular Use for Ladies and Gentlewomen, and all Persons whatsoever that are desirous of being acquainted with the most excellent ARTS of Carving, Cookery, Pastry, Preserving and Laying a Cloth for Grand Entertainments, The like never before extant in any Language. *The book was written by Giles Rose, "one of the Master Cooks in His Majesties Kitchen" and was published in 1682. The enterprising cook is instructed to make the whisk of "fine small twigs of Birch, or such like wood, neatly peeled, and tied up in a quantity a little bigger than your Thumb, and the small ends must be cut off a little, for fear of breaking in your Cream, and so you come to be made ashamed; but for want of Birch take other wood."*

Grasshopper Pie

☆☆☆☆☆☆☆☆☆☆☆☆☆☆☆☆☆

Baked 9-inch or 10-inch
   Chocolate Crumb Crust
   pie shell (see page 117)
30 large marshmallows
½ cup milk
¼ cup crème de menthe
3 tablespoons white crème
   de cacao
1½ cups heavy whipping
   cream
Garnish: Chocolate shavings

The great American dessert tradition includes many, many convenience recipes, such as super-moist cakes that contain pudding mixes, or tomato soup, or sauerkraut. Then there are recipes developed in food manufacturers' kitchens to extend the use of their products, such as Jell-o sponge cakes and Ritz Cracker mock apple pies. I don't know who conceived the idea to replace gelatin with marshmallows in this sweet chiffon that was developed in the 1950s, but it works. The filling is a cloud of mellow mint flavor, resting lightly on a crispy chocolate crust.

☆ ☆ ☆

Prepare the pie shell according to the recipe directions. Cool before filling.

In a heavy-bottomed saucepan over moderate heat, combine the marshmallows and milk and cook, stirring constantly until the marshmallows have melted. Remove from the heat. Cool to room temperature. (Do not refrigerate; the marshmallows will gel if allowed to chill.)

Add the crème de menthe and crème de cacao, beating thoroughly until combined.

Whip the cream until stiff. Fold in the marshmallow mixture. Spoon the filling into the crumb crust. Garnish with chocolate shavings. Chill for 3 to 4 hours or until firm. The pie will hold for up to 24 hours in the refrigerator.

YIELD: 8 TO 10 SERVINGS

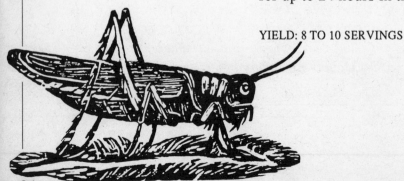

The Modern Priscilla

January 1917   Ten Cents

Tyng

Black Bottom Pie

☆☆☆☆☆☆☆☆☆☆☆☆☆☆☆☆☆

**Baked 9-inch or 10-inch
   Chocolate Crumb Crust
   pie shell (see page 117)**
**2 teaspoons unflavored
   gelatin**
2 tablespoons cold water
4 egg yolks
⅓ cup sugar
4 teaspoons cornstarch
**2 cups hot (not boiling) milk
   or half-and-half**
**3 ounces (½ cup) semi-sweet
   chocolate, finely chopped**
**2 ounces unsweetened
   chocolate, finely chopped**
1 teaspoon vanilla extract
2 tablespoons dark rum
4 egg whites
¼ teaspoon cream of tartar
¼ teaspoon salt
⅓ cup sugar
1 cup heavy whipping cream
Garnish: Chocolate shavings

This pie is heavenly—a dense chocolate bottom topped by a rum-flavored chiffon. Some black bottom aficionados prefer a gingersnap crust, but we like ours with chocolate.

Cool pie shell before filling.

To make the filling, sprinkle the gelatin over the water in a small bowl. Stir and set aside to soften.

In the top part of a double boiler, beat the egg yolks with a wire whisk until thick and lemon colored. Mix in the ⅓ cup sugar and the cornstarch. Place over simmering water. Gradually add the hot milk and cook, stirring constantly, until the mixture lightly coats a metal spoon.

Remove from the heat and measure 1¼ cups of the custard into a small bowl. Add the chopped chocolates. Beat with a fork until smooth. Add the vanilla, cool, and pour into pie crust.

To the remaining hot custard mixture, add the softened gelatin, stirring until dissolved. Mix in the rum. Refrigerate or place the pan in a bowl of ice water, stirring until the mixture mounds slightly when dropped from a spoon. It should be cold, but not set.

Beat the egg whites until foamy. Add the cream of tartar and salt and continue beating until soft peaks form. Gradually add the remaining ⅓ cup sugar and continue beating until stiff and glossy. Gently fold into the custard.

Whip the cream until stiff; fold ½ cup of it into custard mixture, then spread the custard over the chocolate layer. Chill for 3 to 4 hours, or until firm.

Pipe dollops of the remaining whipped cream on top of the pie and sprinkle with chocolate shavings.

YIELD: 8 TO 10 SERVINGS

It takes 4 maple trees, each about 40 years old, to produce enough sap—40 gallons of sap to be exact—to yield 1 gallon of maple syrup.

Maple Chiffon Pie

☆ ☆ ☆ ☆ ☆ ☆ ☆ ☆ ☆ ☆ ☆ ☆ ☆ ☆ ☆ ☆ ☆ ☆

Baked 9-inch pie shell
   (see page 110)
1 envelope unflavored gelatin
¼ cup cold water
3 egg yolks
⅔ cup pure maple syrup
⅓ cup hot milk or half-and-
   half (do not boil)
1 teaspoon vanilla extract
3 egg whites, at room
   temperature
⅛ teaspoon cream of tartar
⅛ teaspoon salt
1 cup heavy whipping cream
¼ cup chopped butternuts
   or walnuts
Garnish: 2 tablespoons finely
   chopped butternuts or
   walnuts

Anyone who has ever tasted maple sap knows how much imagination is required to think that such watery fluid could become sweet syrup. So who thought to boil sap into syrup in the first place? Legend has it that an Iroquois chief by the name of Woksis threw a tomahawk into a maple tree before leaving on a hunt. The weather grew warm that day, and sap flowed from the gash in the tree into a container standing below. The squaw who collected the container thought it was filled with plain water and boiled her evening meat in it. The boiling caused the sap to be reduced to syrup, which gave the meat a whole new flavor, and the rest is history.

☆ ☆ ☆

Prepare the pie shell according to the recipe directions. Bake and let cool on a rack before filling. In a small bowl, sprinkle the gelatin over the cold water. Stir and set aside to soften.

In the top part of a double boiler, beat the egg yolks with a wire whisk until thick and lemon colored. Gradually add the maple syrup and hot milk, mixing until combined. Place the pan over simmering water. Stir constantly until the mixture lightly coats a metal spoon. Add the softened gelatin, stirring until dissolved. Add the vanilla. Refrigerate or place the pan in a bowl of ice water, stirring until the mixture mounds slightly when dropped from a spoon. It should be cold, but not set. Beat the egg whites until foamy. Add the cream of tartar and salt and beat until stiff but not dry. Gently fold into the gelatin mixture.

Beat the cream until stiff. Fold three-fourths of it into the custard, along with the chopped nuts. Spoon into the pie crust. Chill for 3 to 4 hours, or until firm.

Just before serving, pipe the remaining whipped cream on top of the pie. Garnish with chopped nuts.

YIELD: 6 TO 8 SERVINGS

In Vermont, maple sugaring season generally begins in early March, when the days warm up above freezing, but the nights stay cold. This is the optimum weather for a good sap run. Visitors are welcome to most sugar houses, where one is offered (at least) a sip of fresh syrup out of a paper cup. Throughout the state, there are open hours at sugar houses and sugar-on-snow parties, where boiling hot syrup is poured on snow to harden into a sticky candy. The Vermont Maple Festival in St. Albans, in the northwest corner of the state, provides an opportunity to learn how maple syrup is made, enjoy some local Vermont and French Canadian music, and consume a lot of maple syrup in the form of maple cotton candy, maple fudge, maple cream, maple sugar candies, doughnuts and fried dough dunked in syrup, and pancakes.

If Vermont is too far to go, consider visiting Bigo County Park in Indiana, where Maple Sugaring Days are held in February through early March. There you can watch maple syrup being made and enjoy a pancake breakfast.

For more information, contact Vt. Maple Festival Council, Box 255, St. Albans, VT 05478; 802-524-5800 or Maple Sugaring Days, 812-898-2279.

Chocolate Cream Pie

☆☆☆☆☆☆☆☆☆☆☆☆☆☆☆☆☆☆☆☆☆☆

**Baked 9-inch pie shell
  (see page 110)**
1 cup sugar
**¼ cup all-purpose
  unbleached flour**
1 tablespoon cornstarch
¼ teaspoon salt
3 cups milk
**2 ounces unsweetened
  chocolate, chopped**
**2 ounces semi-sweet
  chocolate, chopped,
  or ⅓ cup semi-sweet
  chocolate chips**
4 egg yolks, lightly beaten
**1 tablespoon butter, cut into
  small pieces**
1 tablespoon dark rum
1 teaspoon vanilla extract
1 cup heavy whipping cream
**1 tablespoon sifted
  confectioners sugar**
1 teaspoon dark rum
Garnish: Grated chocolate

What makes a Chocolate Cream Pie so much more wonderful than the chocolate pudding from which it sprang? Undoubtedly, it is the contrast between the crisp crust, the silken chocolate pudding, and the satiny cream topping. This pie speaks of its old-fashioned country origins, of a time when cream and eggs were plentiful and eaten without a sense of sin.

☆☆☆

Prepare the pie shell according to the recipe directions. Bake and let cool on a rack before filling. In a heavy saucepan, combine the sugar, flour, cornstarch, and salt. Add the milk gradually, stirring constantly with a wire whisk to remove any lumps. Add the chopped chocolates. Cook over medium heat, stirring constantly, until the mixture thickens and comes to a boil; continue stirring and boil for 1 minute. Remove from the heat.

Gradually stir a few teaspoons of the pudding mixture into the beaten yolks, mixing constantly until blended. When you have added about ½ cup, pour the yolk mixture back into the pan, stirring until combined. Cook, stirring constantly, for 2 minutes, until thick and smooth. Remove from the heat.

Add the butter gradually. Stir in the 1 tablespoon rum and vanilla. Pour the filling into the baked crust. Cover the surface of the filling with plastic wrap. Let cool. Refrigerate for 3 to 4 hours, or until firm. The pie can be held in the refrigerator for up to 24 hours.

Just before serving, whip the cream until soft peaks form. Add the confectioners sugar and 1 teaspoon rum and beat until stiff. Pipe the whipped cream on top of the pie. Sprinkle with the grated chocolate.

YIELD: 6 TO 8 SERVINGS

Cream pies are associated with the rich bounty of the American Midwest. The first cream pie recipe is probably found in The Improved Housewife, *an 1845 edition by Mrs. A. L. Webster. Her recipe called for 5 eggs, a pint of sweet, thick cream, sugar, raisins, nutmeg, and a pinch of salt.*

Banana Cream Pie

☆ ☆ ☆ ☆ ☆ ☆ ☆ ☆ ☆ ☆ ☆ ☆ ☆ ☆ ☆ ☆ ☆ ☆ ☆

Baked 9-inch pie shell
   (see page 110)
⅔ cup sugar
2 tablespoons all-purpose
   unbleached flour
3 tablespoons cornstarch
¼ teaspoon salt
2 cups milk
4 egg yolks, lightly beaten
2 tablespoons butter, cut into
   small pieces
1 tablespoon dark rum
1 teaspoon vanilla extract
1 cup heavy whipping cream
3 large bananas

Americans consume more bananas than any other fruit, but too few of them, in our opinion, wind up in this luscious dessert. Incidentally, bananas were cultivated by the Arabs in the 7th century. Eight centuries later, in 1482, Portuguese explorers found the fruit growing on the west coast of Africa and picked up the name Guinea natives used for it—banana.

☆ ☆ ☆

Prepare the pie shell according to the recipe directions. Bake and let cool on a rack before filling. In a heavy-bottomed saucepan, combine the sugar, flour, cornstarch, and salt. Add the milk gradually, stirring constantly with a wire whisk to remove any lumps. Cook over medium heat, stirring constantly, until the mixture thickens and comes to a boil. Continue stirring and boil for 1 minute. Remove from the heat.

Gradually stir a few teaspoons of the pudding mixture into the beaten egg yolks, mixing constantly until blended. When you have added about ½ cup, pour the yolk mixture back into the pan, stirring until combined. Cook, stirring constantly, for 2 minutes, until thick and smooth. Remove from the heat.

Add the butter gradually. Stir in the rum and vanilla. Pour into a bowl. Cover the surface of pudding mixture with plastic. Cool completely.

Whip the cream until stiff. Fold half of the whipped cream into the custard filling.

Spoon a thin layer of custard over the bottom of baked pie shell. Arrange a sliced banana over the filling. Alternate layers of custard and bananas, ending with custard. Pipe the remaining whipped cream on top of the pie. Refrigerate the pie for 3 to 4 hours, or until firm.

YIELD: 6 TO 8 SERVINGS

Question: *What food yields the most calories per acre?*

Answer: *Bananas. Within six months of planting, the banana plant is twice as tall as a man. Six months later the fruit begins to form, and in another three or four months it is ready to be harvested. The plant bears only one bunch of fruit, but that bunch will contain about 90 bananas in 9 clusters (some have as many as 140). When the one bunch is cut, the whole plant is chopped down and another one planted. Some varieties can yield from 600 to 800 bunches a year per acre—some 9 million calories, more digestible calories than any other major above-ground crop. Still, bananas aren't the answer to world hunger. To subsist entirely on bananas, a person would have to eat 5 pounds a day.*

Coconut Cream Pie

☆☆☆☆☆☆☆☆☆☆☆☆☆☆☆☆☆☆☆

Baked 9-inch pie shell
  (see page 110)
1 cup sweetened flaked
  coconut
⅔ cup sugar
2 tablespoons all-purpose
  unbleached flour
3 tablespoons cornstarch
¼ teaspoon salt
2 cups milk
4 egg yolks, lightly beaten
2 tablespoons butter, cut into
  small pieces
1½ teaspoons vanilla extract
1 tablespoon Apricot Glaze
  (see page 118)
4 egg whites, at room
  temperature
½ teaspoon cream of tartar
Pinch salt
½ cup sugar
1 teaspoon vanilla extract
½ cup sweetened, flaked
  coconut for garnish

The coconut followed the banana as a tropical fruit that met wide acceptance in America. Its introduction was serendipitous.

In 1895, a Cuban businessman found himself in debt to a Philadelphia miller by the name of Franklin Baker. In lieu of a cash payment, the Cuban shipped north a cargo-load of fresh coconuts.

What does an enterprising businessman do with a load of coconuts? Baker figured that the market was wide open—if he could somehow make using coconuts easier. Determined to make a go of the coconut business, Baker found machinery with which to process the coconut meat, installed shredders, and began to package the convenient dried flakes for sale in grocery stores. Within 2 years he sold his flour mills and gave full time to the new enterprise—Baker's Coconut.

☆ ☆ ☆

Prepare the pie shell according to the recipe directions. Bake and let cool on a rack before filling.

Preheat the oven to 300° F. Toast the 1 cup of the coconut on a baking sheet for 10 minutes, stirring or shaking the pan occasionally. Set aside.

In a heavy-bottomed saucepan, combine the ⅔ cup sugar, flour, cornstarch, and salt. Add the milk gradually, stirring constantly with a wire whisk to remove any lumps. Cook over medium heat, stirring constantly until the mixture thickens and comes to a boil. Continue stirring and boil for 1 minute. Remove from the heat.

Gradually stir a few teaspoons of the pudding mixture into the beaten egg yolks, mixing constantly until blended. When you have added about ½ cup, pour the yolk mixture back into pan, stirring until combined. Cook, stirring constantly, for 2 minutes, until thick and smooth. Remove from the heat.

Add the butter gradually. Stir in the 1½ teaspoons vanilla. Mix in the toasted coconut. Brush the baked pie shell with the apricot glaze. Pour in the filling. Prepare the meringue immediately.

Preheat the oven to 375° F.

In the large bowl of an electric mixer, beat the egg whites until foamy. Add the cream of tartar and salt and beat until soft peaks form. Gradually sprinkle in the remaining ½ cup sugar, 1 tablespoon at a time, beating well after each addition. When all the sugar has been incorporated, add the remaining 1 teaspoon vanilla and beat well for 3 to 4 more minutes, until the meringue forms stiff, shiny peaks.

Place about half of the meringue around the edge of the warm filling. Use a rubber spatula to carefully seal it to the pie crust. Pile the remaining meringue in the center, then spread with the back of a spoon to make decorative swirls. Sprinkle with the remaining ½ cup untoasted coconut. Bake for 7 to 8 minutes, or until the meringue and coconut are golden brown. Cool on a rack in a draft-free place. Serve at room temperature. This pie tastes best when eaten within 3 hours after cooling. Refrigerate any leftover pie.

YIELD: 6 TO 8 SERVINGS

Lemon Meringue Pie

☆ ☆ ☆ ☆ ☆ ☆ ☆ ☆ ☆ ☆ ☆ ☆ ☆ ☆ ☆ ☆ ☆ ☆ ☆ ☆

Baked 9-inch pie shell
 (see page 110)
4 egg yolks
1¼ cups sugar
6 tablespoons cornstarch
⅛ teaspoon salt
1½ cups water
½ cup fresh lemon juice
2 tablespoons butter,
 cut into small pieces
1 tablespoon lemon zest
4 egg whites, at room
 temperature
½ teaspoon cream of tartar
Pinch of salt
½ cup sugar
2 teaspoons lemon zest

Who could fail to sing the praises of a billowy tall lemon meringue pie? The tangy, silken lemon base is the perfect counterpoint to the airy cloud of sweet meringue. This pie was the epitome of the American-style haute cuisine that was practiced in New York and Philadelphia in the mid to late 1800s. Part of the appeal in those days was its expense—the excessive number of eggs, the refined sugar, fresh imported lemons, and sweet creamery butter. Incidently, if you ever find an old recipe for vinegar pie, what you would be looking at would be a poor man's lemon meringue. In that recipe, cider vinegar and the zest of half a lemon replace the fresh lemons. But we accept no substitutes here: This old-fashioned pie tastes as good as ever.

☆ ☆ ☆

Prepare the pie shell according to the recipe directions. Bake and cool on a rack before filling.

To prepare the lemon filling, beat the egg yolks lightly in a small bowl. Set aside.

In the top part of a double boiler, combine the 1¼ cups sugar, cornstarch, and ⅛ teaspoon salt. Gradually stir in the water and lemon juice. Place the double boiler over (not in) simmering water. Using a whisk, stir the mixture constantly until the sugar is dissolved and the mixture thickens and just comes to a boil. Remove from the heat. Gradually stir a few teaspoons of the pudding mixture into the beaten egg yolks, mixing constantly until blended. When you have added about ½ cup, pour the yolk mixture back into the pan, stirring constantly until combined.

Place the pan over the simmering water again. Whisk in the butter gradually, then the 1 tablespoon lemon zest. Cook over low heat, stirring constantly, for 10 minutes or until the mixture is thick and smooth. Remove from the heat. Stir to cool slightly, then pour into the baked pie shell.

Preheat the oven to 375° F. and prepare the meringue immediately.

In the large bowl of an electric mixer, beat the egg whites until foamy. Add the cream of tartar and pinch of salt and beat until soft peaks form. Gradually sprinkle in the remaining ½ cup sugar, 1 tablespoon at a time, beating well after each addition. When all the sugar has been incorporated, add the remaining 2 teaspoons of lemon rind and beat well for 3 to 4 more minutes, until the meringue forms stiff, shiny peaks.

Place about half of the meringue around the edge of the warm filling. Use a rubber spatula to carefully seal it to the pie crust. Pile the remaining meringue in the center, then spread with the back of a spoon to make decorative swirls. Bake for 7 to 8 minutes, or until the meringue is a golden brown. Cool on a rack in a draft-free place. Serve at room temperature. This pie tastes best when eaten within 3 hours after cooling. Refrigerate any leftover pie.

YIELD: 6 TO 8 SERVINGS

Key Lime Pie

☆☆☆☆☆☆☆☆☆☆☆☆☆☆☆

**Baked 9-inch pie shell
  (see page 110)**
3 egg yolks
**1 (14-ounce) can sweetened
  condensed milk**
1 tablespoon lime zest
**½ cup lime juice (preferably
  key lime juice, fresh or
  bottled; if key lime juice
  isn't available, use fresh
  lime juice from regular
  limes)**
**3 egg whites, at room
  temperature**
¼ teaspoon cream of tartar
⅛ teaspoon salt
¼ cup sugar
**1 cup heavy whipping cream,
  whipped (optional)**

In 1883, Gail Borden applied for a patent on his process of preserving milk. He boiled off the water in the milk in an airtight vaccum pan, similar to those he had seen used by Shakers for condensing sweetened fruit juices. The heat process and the added sugar preserved the milk by inhibiting the activity of bacteria. It took consumers many years to trust Borden's condensed milk, the "milk that would stay sweet." But after the Civil War it was a godsend to the South, where years of battle and plunder had devastated its agricultural base. In Key West, Florida, sweetened condensed milk was not only a sorely needed food, it was the inspiration for the famous Key Lime Pie.

☆ ☆ ☆

Prepare the pie shell according to the recipe directions. Bake and cool on a rack before filling. Preheat the oven to 325° F.

In a mixing bowl, beat the egg yolks with a rotary beater or electric mixer for 3 to 4 minutes until thick and lemon colored. Gradually add the condensed milk, beating until blended. Then add the lime zest and lime juice; continue beating until thick and smooth.

In another bowl, beat the egg whites until foamy. Add the cream of tartar and salt and beat until soft peaks form. Add the sugar gradually and beat until stiff but not dry. The egg whites should hold their shape and remain moist. Fold the whites into the lime mixture. Spoon the mixture into the pie shell.

Bake for 20 minutes or until the filling is set and just beginning to turn golden. Cool on a rack. Refrigerate the pie for 3 to 4 hours, or until firm. Just before serving, pipe whipped cream on top or serve the whipped cream separately.

YIELD: 6 TO 8 SERVINGS

Rolling Pins

Rolling pins were not always the cylindrical affairs they are today. In Southern plantation kitchens of the 1700s, the rolling pin had a large U-shaped handle that could be grasped in the middle and operated with one hand. This left the other hand free to work the dough—an improvement on the rolling pin design of today.

Basic Pie Crust

☆ ☆ ☆ ☆ ☆ ☆ ☆ ☆ ☆ ☆ ☆ ☆ ☆ ☆ ☆ ☆ ☆

2½ cups all-purpose unbleached flour
½ teaspoon salt
½ cup chilled butter, cut into small pieces
6 tablespoons solid vegetable shortening (chill the shortening if you are using a food processor)
6 tablespoons ice water, or more if needed

I n the old days, this recipe would have required lard, or a combination of butter and lard, and the result would have been excellent—a tender, flaky crust, albeit one that is somewhat higher in cholesterol. Lard is still available in the dairy case and you can substitute it—at your own risk—for the vegetable shortening.

This recipe makes enough dough for 1 double crust pie, or 2 single crust pie shells. If you need just 1 pie shell, you can halve the recipe, or make 2 pie shells and freeze the second one.

☆ ☆ ☆

Mixing By Hand

Combine the flour and salt in a large mixing bowl. With a pastry blender or 2 knives, cut in the butter. Then add the shortening and combine until the particles are the size of small peas. While stirring lightly and quickly with a fork, sprinkle with water, 1 tablespoon at a time, just until all the flour is moistened. If dough doesn't hold together when squeezed, sprinkle with additional water until it holds together and does not crumble. If the dough is sticky, sprinkle with a little more flour. Using the heel of your hand, press portions of the dough flat against your work surface. This will help to distribute the fat and make the dough easier to roll out. Reshape the dough and flatten it into 2 disks (if you are making a double crust pie, make one disk slightly larger than the other) and dust with flour. Wrap separately in plastic film wrap. Chill for at least 30 minutes or up to 4 days in the refrigerator.

Mixing in a Food Processor

Combine the flour and salt in a food processor fitted with a metal blade. Add the shortening and butter and process with on-and-off pulses until the mixture has the consistency of coarse meal.

Add 1 tablespoon of ice water through the feed tube, then pulse for 3 seconds. Repeat this start-and-stop procedure with additional tablespoons of water. Process this mixture until it just begins to stick together, but do not allow it to form a ball. Turn the dough out onto a sheet of plastic, pull up on the corners to form a ball, and then shape and press the mixture together to form 2 flattened disks. (If you are making a double crust pie, make one disk slightly larger than the other.) Dust with flour and wrap separately in plastic film wrap. Chill for at least 30 minutes or up to 4 days in the refrigerator.

Rolling, Shaping, and Baking a Single Crust Pie Shell

If the dough has chilled for several hours, remove it from the refrigerator and leave at room temperature for 15 minutes so it will be easier to handle.

On a lightly floured pastry cloth or board, roll out the dough into a circle, rolling from center to edge in an even, light stroke. Work quickly to handle the dough as little as possible. Roll the dough to a thickness of a little less than ⅛ inch and 2 inches larger than the inverted pie plate. Fold the circle in half, lift off the board, and lay the fold across the center of pie plate or tart pan. Unfold and ease the dough loosely into place without stretching it.

Trim the overhanging edge ½ inch larger than the outside rim of plate. Fold it under, even with the rim of the pie plate and crimp or flute the edge. Refrigerate the pie shell for 15 minutes.

Then fill and bake as directed in a recipe or bake unfilled. For **a fully baked pie shell**, preheat the oven to 425° F. Remove the pie dough from the refrigerator and prick the bottom and sides of dough with a fork at ½-inch intervals. Fit a large circle of foil into the bottom and up the sides of the pie dough. Fill it with

dried beans or baker's pellets to provide weight and prevent the crust from buckling.

Bake in lower third of the oven for 10 minutes, then remove the foil and beans. Prick the bottom of crust with a fork again to keep it from puffing up. Return the pie shell to the oven for 10 to 12 minutes, or until it is golden. Cool on a rack before filling.

For a **partially baked pie shell**, preheat the oven to 425° F. Remove the pie shell from the refrigerator, but do not prick the crust. Line the pastry with a circle of foil and weight with dried beans or baker's pellets to prevent buckling.

Bake in the lower third of the oven for 10 minutes, or until the pastry is set. Remove the foil and beans and bake for 3 to 4 minutes longer, or until pie shell just begins to color. Cool on a rack before filling.

Rolling and Shaping Dough for a Double Crust Pie

If the dough has chilled for several hours, remove it from the refrigerator and leave at room temperature for 15 minutes so it will be easier to handle.

To make the bottom crust, place the larger disk of chilled dough on a lightly floured pastry cloth or board and roll it out into a circle, rolling from the center to the edge in even, light strokes. Work quickly to handle the dough as little as possible. Roll the dough to a thickness of a little less than ⅛ inch and 2 inches larger than the inverted pie plate. Fold the circle in half, lift it off the board, and lay the fold across the center of the pie plate. Unfold and ease the dough loosely into place without stretching it. Trim the overhanging edge even with the rim of the pie plate. Fill the pie shell with the desired filling.

To make the top crust, roll out the remaining dough into a circle about 1 inch larger than the pie plate. Moisten the edge of the bottom crust with water. Fold the dough circle in half, lift off

112

the board, place it across the center of filled pie, and unfold. Trim the edge ½ inch larger than the pie plate and tuck the overhang under the edge of bottom crust. Crimp the edges together with a fork or make a fluted pattern with your fingers. Make several decorative slits into the top crust to allow steam to escape. Refrigerate the pie for 15 minutes. Bake as directed in the recipe used.

Sweet Pastry Crust Variation

To make a sweet pastry dough, add 2 tablespoons of sugar to the flour and salt mixture. For a variation in flavor, use half orange juice and half water for the liquid.

YIELD: 1 DOUBLE CRUST FOR AN 8-INCH OR 9-INCH PIE
        OR TWO 9-INCH SINGLE CRUSTS

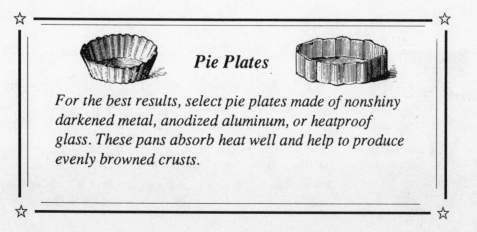

Pie Plates

For the best results, select pie plates made of nonshiny darkened metal, anodized aluminum, or heatproof glass. These pans absorb heat well and help to produce evenly browned crusts.

Cream Cheese Pastry

☆☆☆☆☆☆☆☆☆☆☆☆☆☆☆☆☆☆☆☆☆☆☆

1 cup all-purpose
   unbleached flour
⅛ teaspoon salt
3 ounces cream cheese
½ cup butter or margarine,
   cut into small pieces

Here's a rich pastry that makes a wonderful single crust pie shell. Double the recipe if you want a double-crust pie.

Combine the flour and salt by hand or in a food processor fitted with a steel blade. Add the cream cheese and butter and process, or use a pastry blender to cut in the cream cheese and butter, until the mixture has the consistency of coarse meal. Turn the dough out onto a floured board and knead lightly, just until the dough holds together. Shape the dough into a ball, then flatten into a disk. Dust with flour. Wrap in plastic and chill while you prepare the filling.

If the dough has chilled for several hours, remove it from the refrigerator and leave at room temperature for 15 minutes so it will be easier to handle.

On a lightly floured pastry cloth or board, roll out the dough into a circle, rolling from center to edge in an even, light stroke. Work quickly to handle the dough as little as possible. Roll the dough to a thickness of a little less than ⅛ inch and 2 inches larger than the inverted pie plate. Fold the circle in half, lift off the board, and lay the fold across the center of pie plate or tart pan. Unfold and ease the dough loosely into place without stretching it.

Trim the overhanging edge ½ inch larger than the outside rim of plate. Fold it under, even with the rim of the pie plate and crimp or flute the edge. Refrigerate the pie shell for 15 minutes.

Then fill and bake as directed in a recipe or bake unfilled. For a **fully baked pie shell**, preheat the oven to 425° F. Remove the pie dough from the refrigerator and prick the bottom and sides of dough with a fork at ½-inch intervals. Fit a large circle of foil into the bottom and up the sides of the pie dough. Fill it with dried beans or baker's pellets to provide weight and prevent the

crust from buckling.

Bake in lower third of the oven for 10 minutes, then remove the foil and beans. Prick the bottom of crust with a fork again to keep it from puffing up. Return the pie shell to the oven for 10 to 12 minutes, or until it is golden. Cool on a rack before filling.

For a **partially baked pie shell**, preheat the oven to 425° F. Remove the pie shell from the refrigerator, but do not prick the crust. Line the pastry with a circle of foil and weight with dried beans or baker's pellets to prevent buckling.

Bake in the lower third of the oven for 10 minutes, or until the pastry is set. Remove the foil and beans and bake for 3 to 4 minutes longer, or until pie shell just begins to color. Cool on a rack before filling.

YIELD: 1 SINGLE-CRUST PIE SHELL

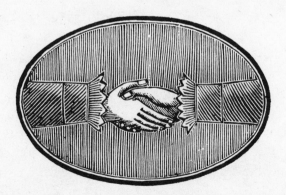

Graham Cracker Crust

☆ ☆ ☆ ☆ ☆ ☆ ☆ ☆ ☆ ☆ ☆ ☆ ☆ ☆ ☆ ☆ ☆ ☆ ☆ ☆

**1½ cups finely ground
graham cracker crumbs
3 tablespoons sugar
6 tablespoons butter or
margarine, melted
¼ teaspoon cinnamon**

To save time, some people don't bother to bake crumb crusts. But we find that baking results in a pie that is less soggy, cuts better, and has a nice toasty flavor.

Preheat the oven to 350° F. Lightly grease an 8-inch or 9-inch pie plate or springform pan.

Combine the graham cracker crumbs, sugar, butter, and cinnamon. Press firmly into bottom and up the sides of the pan. Bake for 8 minutes. Set aside on a rack to cool before filling.

YIELD: 8-INCH OR 9-INCH PIE SHELL

Chocolate Crumb Crust

☆ ☆

**1¾ cups finely ground
chocolate wafer crumbs
5 tablespoons butter or
margarine, melted**

Preheat the oven to 350° F. Lightly grease an 8-inch or 9-inch pie plate or springform pan.
Combine the crumbs and melted butter. Press firmly onto the bottom and up the sides of the pan. Bake for 8 minutes. Set aside on a rack to cool before filling.

YIELD: 9-INCH OR 10-INCH PIE SHELL

Family Pie-Crust

Take one cup of nice drippings and mix with goose, duck or chicken fat. In the fall and winter, when poultry is plentiful and fat, you should save all drippings for pie-crust. If you have neither of the above, use rendered meat fat (I do not mean suet—that is horrid!—but genuine meat fat); use half butter; if you consider this "Trefa" use all fat. Take one cup of fat, stir to a cream, add a salt-spoonful of salt, four cups of sifted flour, rub creamed fat and flour between your hands until it looks like sand; make a hole in the center, pour in a cupful of ice water and mix lightly, do not knead and it will be flaky. This will make four pies. You may keep the dough in your refrigerator for a week. Bake pies fresh every day; they are quickly made when the dough is ready.

"Aunt Babette's" Cook Book (Cincinnati and Chicago: The Bloch Publishing and Printing Co., 1891).

Apricot Glaze

☆ ☆ ☆ ☆ ☆ ☆ ☆ ☆ ☆ ☆ ☆ ☆ ☆ ☆ ☆ ☆

1 cup apricot preserves
2 tablespoons brandy

This glaze can be used to seal the bottom crust on fruit pies, top a cake, or glaze fruit on a tart. If you like, serve a dollop of the glaze on top of baked custard.

☆ ☆ ☆

Combine the preserves and brandy in a small saucepan. Stir over low heat until the jam has melted. Strain and cool. Store extra in the refrigerator.

YIELD: 1 CUP

Fruit Desserts

☆☆☆☆☆☆☆☆☆☆☆☆☆☆☆☆☆☆☆☆☆☆

Apple Crisp

☆☆☆☆☆☆☆☆☆☆☆☆

Filling

3 pounds tart apples, peeled,
   cored, and sliced
   (about 7 cups)
1 tablespoon lemon zest
1 tablespoon lemon juice
¼ cup white sugar
1 teaspoon cinnamon
½ teaspoon nutmeg

Topping

½ cup all-purpose
   unbleached flour
½ cup firmly packed dark
   brown sugar
½ cup ground cookie or
   graham cracker crumbs
½ cup butter or margarine,
   at room temperature
⅓ cup chopped almonds

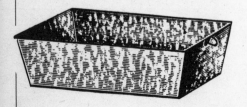

Apple crisp, apple crunch, apple delight—there were, and are, many names for this dessert with an apple pie filling and a crunchy topping, and many variations. This sort of dessert was widespread in early American kitchens because it was perfect to make with the less-than-perfect apples that were dug up from bins in the root cellar. After all the worm holes and bruises were cut away, baked apples were out of the question, perhaps, but apple crisp, crunch, delight was just the thing.

☆☆☆

Preheat the oven to 350° F. Lightly grease a 9-inch square baking dish or a deep 9-inch pie plate.

Place the apples in the baking dish. Toss with the lemon rind, lemon juice, sugar, cinnamon, and nutmeg. Rearrange the apples, pressing down on them so that they're level with the top of the dish.

In a bowl, combine the flour, brown sugar, and cookie crumbs. With your fingers, rub the butter into the crumb mixture until it resembles coarse meal. Mix in the almonds. Sprinkle the topping over the apples, pressing it down and making sure the edges are covered.

Bake for 45 minutes or until the top is browned and the apples are tender when tested with a fork.

Serve warm or chilled with cream, whipped cream, or ice cream.

YIELD: 6 SERVINGS

In short, if you wish to avail yourself of the blessings of a bountiful Providence, which are within your reach, you must plant an orchard. And when you do it, see that you plant good fruit. The best are cheapest.

McCalls' *Home Cook Book and General Guide*. Compiled by Mrs. Jennie Harlan (New York: The McCall Company, 1890).

Cherry Crunch

☆☆☆☆☆☆☆☆☆☆☆☆☆☆☆☆

2 cups drained and pitted
   canned cherries
   (reserve ½ cup cherry
   juice) or 2 cups defrosted
   frozen cherries, drained
   (reserve juice and add
   additional grape or orange
   juice to make ½ cup)
1½ tablespoons Minute brand
   tapioca
1 cup all-purpose
   unbleached flour
¼ teaspoon baking powder
¼ teaspoon baking soda
¼ teaspoon salt
1 cup brown sugar
1 cup rolled oats (not instant)
½ cup butter or margarine, at
   room temperature
½ cup chopped walnuts
¼ teaspoon almond extract

Here the cherries are sandwiched between a coarse-textured, brown sugar pastry. In the finished dish, the cherries appear as bumps pressing up on the crust.

☆ ☆ ☆

In a small bowl, mix ½ cup of the cherry juice with the tapioca, stirring to combine. Set aside for 15 minutes.

Preheat the oven to 350° F.

In a bowl, combine the flour, baking powder, baking soda, salt, and brown sugar. Stir in the oats. With your fingertips, rub the butter into the dry ingredients until it resembles coarse meal. Stir in the walnuts.

Press half of the crumb mixture into the bottom of a 9-inch square baking dish. Arrange the cherries over it. Add the almond extract to the tapioca mixture and spoon over the cherries. Cover the fruit with the remaining crumb mixture.

Bake for 35 to 40 minutes or until golden brown. Serve warm or chilled with cream, whipped cream, or vanilla ice cream.

YIELD: 6 SERVINGS

A cherry year, a merry year
A plum year, a dumb year

123

Apple Brown Betty

☆☆☆☆☆☆☆☆☆☆☆☆☆☆☆☆☆☆

1 cup dry unseasoned bread
    crumbs
¼ cup white sugar
⅓ cup melted butter
5 cups peeled and sliced
    apples (5 to 6
    medium-size apples)
½ cup brown sugar
1 teaspoon cinnamon
½ teaspoon nutmeg
Zest and juice of
    1 lemon
½ cup chopped walnuts

This is one of the simplest of the fruit desserts, and we have no idea of how the name originated. The addition of the walnuts adds extra flavor and texture.

☆ ☆ ☆

Preheat the oven to 350° F. Lightly butter a 1½-quart baking dish.

Combine the bread crumbs with the white sugar and butter. Pat half of the mixture in the bottom of the baking dish.

Combine the apples, brown sugar, cinnamon, nutmeg, lemon juice and zest, and walnuts. Spread over the crumbs. Top with the remaining crumbs. Cover and bake for 40 minutes. Then remove the cover, increase the heat to 400° F., and continue to bake for 10 more minutes. Serve warm with cream, whipped cream, or ice cream.

YIELD: 6 SERVINGS

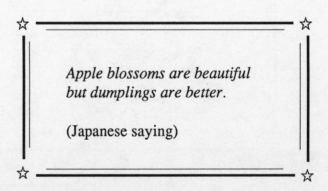

Apple blossoms are beautiful but dumplings are better.

(Japanese saying)

Apple Dumplings

☆ ☆ ☆ ☆ ☆ ☆ ☆ ☆ ☆ ☆ ☆ ☆ ☆ ☆ ☆ ☆

2 cups all-purpose unbleached flour
2 tablespoons sugar
½ teaspoon salt
¼ cup solid vegetable shortening
½ cup butter
Ice water
6 large baking apples
¼ cup butter, at room temperature
¼ cup raspberry or black-berry preserves
¼ cup chopped almonds
2 teaspoons orange zest
1 egg white, slightly beaten

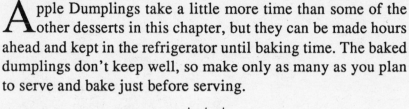

Apple Dumplings take a little more time than some of the other desserts in this chapter, but they can be made hours ahead and kept in the refrigerator until baking time. The baked dumplings don't keep well, so make only as many as you plan to serve and bake just before serving.

☆ ☆ ☆

Preheat the oven to 400° F. Lightly butter a large shallow baking dish.

Combine the flour, sugar, and salt in a mixing bowl or in a food processor fitted with a steel blade. Cut in the shortening and butter until the mixture resembles coarse crumbs. Add just enough ice water to allow the mixture to hold together. Divide into 6 balls and flatten into disks. Chill while you prepare the filling.

Peel the apples and core about three-quarters of the way down. Trim the bottoms, if necessary, to allow the apples to stand.

Beat together the butter and preserves. Mix in the almonds and orange zest. Stuff into the apple cores.

On a lightly floured board, roll out each pastry disk to a square of approximately 6 inches. Brush with the egg white and center an apple on each square. Bring the dough up over the apple and press the edges together, using egg white if needed to make them stick. If you want to get fancy, use scraps of dough to make apple leaves, and affix on top of the dumplings with a little egg white. Place in the prepared baking dish.

Chill for several hours in the refrigerator, or for 3 to 5 minutes in the freezer. Then place in the preheated oven and bake for 45 minutes, until the tops are golden brown. Serve warm with whipped cream or ice cream.

YIELD: 6 SERVINGS

In one word, Queequeg, said I, rather digressively; hell is an idea first born on an undigested apple dumpling; and since then perpetrated through the hereditary dyspepsias nurtured by Ramadans.

Herman Melville, *Moby-Dick* (1851)

Apple Pandowdy

☆☆☆☆☆☆☆☆☆☆☆☆☆☆☆

Pastry

1¼ cups all-purpose
    unbleached flour
⅓ cup cornmeal
2 tablespoons sugar
¼ teaspoon salt
¼ cup solid vegetable
    shortening
⅓ cup butter
Approximately ¼ cup ice
    water

Apple Filling

6 cups peeled and sliced
    apples (6 to 8 apples)
1½ teaspoons cinnamon
½ teaspoon mace
⅓ cup pure maple syrup
¼ cup melted butter
¼ cup apple cider or juice
¼ cup light cream
2 tablespoons pure maple
    syrup
2 tablespoons melted butter

A pandowdy is a cross between a pie and a pudding. With a filling that includes butter and a little cream, it is richer than your average pie. This old-fashioned dessert is obviously for those of us with old-fashioned work habits. Serve after a hard day in the garden, chopping wood, or running a marathon.

☆ ☆ ☆

Combine the flour, cornmeal, sugar, and salt in a mixing bowl or in a food processor fitted with a steel blade. Cut in the shortening and butter until the mixture resembles coarse crumbs. Add just enough ice water to allow the mixture to hold together. Divide into 2 balls and flatten into disks. Chill while you prepare the filling.

Preheat the oven to 400° F.

Combine the apples with the cinnamon, mace, ⅓ cup maple syrup, and ¼ cup melted butter.

Roll out one piece of dough about ⅛ inch thick to fit into a 1½-quart baking dish. Place in the dish and trim the uneven edges. The dough should fit up the sides of the baking dish, but don't worry if it doesn't.

Spoon the apples into the baking dish, scraping out the syrup and butter in the bottom of the bowl. Roll out the second piece of dough and fit over the apples. Seal against the sides of the dish.

Place in the preheated oven and bake for about 10 minutes. Remove the pandowdy from the oven and reduce the heat to 325°. Using a sharp knife or a chopper, cut the crust into the fruit, until the crust has almost disappeared into the fruit. Combine the apple cider, cream, the remaining 2 tablespoons maple syrup, and remaining 2 tablespoons melted butter. Pour over the top. Return to the oven and continue to bake for 45 to 50 minutes. Remove from the oven and serve warm.

YIELD: 6 SERVINGS

NEW LINE BETWEEN
ALBANY & NEWBURG

LANDING AT

Hamburgh, Marlborough, Milton, Poughkeepsie, Hyde Park, Kingston, Rhinebeck, Barrytown, Redhook, Bristol, Westcamp Catskill, Hudson, Coxsackie, Stuyvesant, Baltimore & Coeymans.

On and after *MONDAY*, October 15th,

The Superior Low Pressure Steamer

ST. NICHOLAS

CAPTAIN WILSON,

Will run as a Passage and Freight Boat between Newburgh and Albany, leaving Newburgh

MONDAYS, WEDNESDAYS & FRIDAYS

AT SEVEN O'CLOCK A.M.,

And ALBANY on Tuesdays, Thursdays & Saturdays, at half-past 9 o'clock A.M.

Albany, Oct. 9th, 1849.

Berry Cobbler

☆☆☆☆☆☆☆☆☆☆☆☆☆☆☆

Berry Filling

6 cups fresh blackberries,
  boysenberries,
  raspberries, blueberries,
  or a combination of
  berries
3 tablespoons flour
½ cup sugar or to taste
2 teaspoons orange zest
1 tablespoon orange juice
2 tablespoons butter, cut into
  small pieces

Biscuit Dough Topping

1 cup all-purpose
  unbleached flour
1½ teaspoons baking powder
2 tablespoons sugar
¼ teaspoon salt
3 tablespoons chilled butter,
  cut into small pieces
1 tablespoon solid vegetable
  shortening
¼ to ⅓ cup milk or
  half-and-half
1 tablespoon melted butter
1 tablespoon sugar

Yet another variation on the biscuit and fruit theme. The name probably derives from an old Middle English word that means "to lump together." It also means, according to Webster, "to make or do clumsily or unhandily." Well, this lumped together dish of biscuit and fruit tastes lovely, no matter what its name or homely appearance. We've always thought the rough, uneven surface of the biscuit topping reminded us of cobblestones.

☆ ☆ ☆

Stem and gently rinse the berries. Drain on paper towels, then place in an 8-inch square baking dish or 1½-quart casserole. In a small bowl, combine the 3 tablespoons of flour, ½ cup sugar, and orange zest and juice. Toss with the berries, mixing gently until they are thoroughly coated. Dot with the 2 tablespoons of butter. Set aside for 30 minutes or refrigerate for several hours. Bring to room temperature before baking.

Preheat the oven to 400° F.

To make the biscuit dough, sift together the flour, baking powder, 2 tablespoons sugar, and salt into a bowl. With a pastry blender or with your fingertips, cut or rub the butter and shortening into the dry ingredients until the mixture has the consistency of coarse crumbs. Add ¼ cup of the milk all at once and stir with a fork just until the dough comes together, adding more milk if necessary.

Turn the dough out onto a lightly floured pastry cloth or board. Knead lightly for about 12 to 15 times, sprinkling with a little flour if the dough is sticky. Biscuit dough can be refrigerated for up to 2 hours before baking. Press the dough out gently into a shape that will be large enough to cover berries. Transfer the dough carefully to the baking dish, crimping the edges around the dish. Brush the top of the dough with melted butter. Sprinkle with the remaining 1 tablespoon sugar. With the tip of a sharp knife, cut 3 to 4 vents in the top of the dough to allow steam to escape.

Bake for 35 to 40 minutes, or until the crust is golden. Serve warm with a spoonful of heavy cream.

YIELD: 6 SERVINGS

You may make houses enchantingly beautiful, hang them with pictures, have them clean and airy and convenient; but if the stomach is fed with sour bread and burnt meats, it will raise such rebellions that the eyes will see no beauty anywhere.

The House-keepers Manual by Catherine E. Beecher and Harriet Beecher Stow (Cincinnati: J. B.Ford & Co., 1874).

Peach Slump

☆☆☆☆☆☆☆☆☆☆☆☆☆☆☆☆

8 cups thinly sliced peeled
    peaches (approximately 8
    medium-size peaches)
2 tablespoons light brown
    sugar
½ teaspoon almond extract
½ teaspoon cinnamon
1½ cups all-purpose
    unbleached flour
2 teaspoons baking powder
2 tablespoons white sugar
⅓ cup butter
½ cup milk
¼ cup buttermilk or plain
    yogurt
1 egg, well beaten

Many of our heritage fruit dessert recipes are variations on a single theme—fruit and biscuit dough—and this slump is no exception. Here peaches are baked under a biscuit topping, but then the dessert is inverted onto a serving plate so the fruit can "slump" into the pastry. You can further the slumping process by whacking the fruit with a spoon, as some recipes recommend, but we prefer to skip that step. Serve this as soon after you remove it from the oven as possible. After it has sat around for a couple of hours, the biscuit dough becomes pasty. Nectarines or apples can be substituted for the peaches.

☆ ☆ ☆

Preheat the oven to 400° F. Lightly butter a 1½-quart casserole.

In a medium-size bowl, toss together the peaches, brown sugar, almond extract, and cinnamon. Spread in the bottom of the casserole.

Sift together the flour, baking powder, and 2 tablespoons of the white sugar. Cut the butter into the flour mixture, until it has the consistency of coarse crumbs. Combine the milk, buttermilk or yogurt, and egg and combine with the flour. Do not knead; the dough will be sticky, stiff, and lumpy. Drop by the spoonful over the peaches. Try to get even coverage, but don't worry about a few bare spots. Bake for about 25 minutes, until the top is golden and the juices are bubbling. Cool on a wire rack for about 5 minutes. Then loosen the biscuit from the sides of the pan and invert onto a serving platter.

YIELD: 4 TO 6 SERVINGS

One of the easiest and most effective ways to cut butter into flour is to grate chilled or frozen butter into the flour and then briefly work it in with your hands. The resulting biscuit should be very flaky.

133

Blueberry Grunt

☆☆☆☆☆☆☆☆☆☆☆☆☆☆☆☆☆☆☆☆

**6 cups fresh or unsweetened
frozen blueberries
1 cup water
1½ cups sugar
½ teaspoon cinnamon
1¾ cups unbleached
all-purpose flour
½ teaspoon salt
1 tablespoon baking powder
6 tablespoons butter
Approximately ¾ cup milk**

One can easily imagine how this recipe came about. On a hot August day in Maine, a cook, planning to make a blueberry shortcake, decided it was just too hot to fire up the woodstove for the shortcake biscuits. So instead, she put the blueberries in a pot with some sugar and water and steamed the biscuit dough like dumplings, hoping for the best.

The first time I made this, I was hoping for the best, too. The look of this dessert is completely unpromising. Indeed, my heart sank when I saw the gluey looking biscuits. But, this dessert is my absolute favorite. Serve it up in the kitchen in dessert bowls and cover with a slosh of unsweetened cream. The flavor, the contrast of textures—it's divine.

In a 9-inch or 10-inch nonreactive skillet, combine the berries, water, sugar, and cinnamon. Bring to a boil, then simmer for 10 minutes. Remove from the heat while you prepare the biscuit dough.

Sift together the flour, salt, and baking powder. Cut in the butter until the mixture resembles coarse crumbs. Make a well in the center and pour in the milk. Mix just enough to combine. Drop by the spoonful over the berries. Cover tightly and steam for 15 to 20 minutes, keeping the heat just high enough to allow the berries to bubble.

Serve warm in bowls with unsweetened cream.

YIELD: 6 SERVINGS

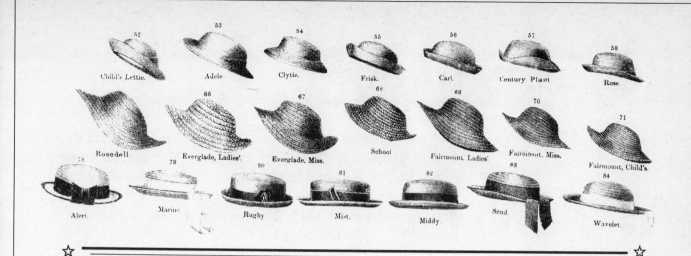

The high-bush blueberry is a charming plant. It grows, thorn-free, to convenient picking heights. Its plump, dusky blue berries glisten like jewels in the morning dew. I have picked such berries at pick-your-own farms, stripping a bush with clumsy fingers and filling a bucket hung from a nylon cord around my neck in minutes. It was easy, too easy, in fact.

No high-bush blueberry can compare to the taste of a wild low-bush blueberry. Picking these tiny berries that grow on ankle-high shrubs is hard labor. Professionals — meaning those seasonal workers who are paid for their efforts with cash, not muffins — use a rake to strip the low-growing shrubs of the berries. But the work is back-breaking, and yields are relatively low. Most of the commercial harvest goes into commercial baking, where the small berries are prized for muffins. Still some of the wild blueberry crop makes it to farmstands and fruit markets in New England.

Wild is something of a misnomer. The berries are wild only in so far as the fields are not planted by the farmer. But they are managed. After harvest each year, the farmer burns the fields to eliminate weeds. Underground, the blueberry rhizomes remain intact, ready to spread to the newly cleared grounds. Birds help the process by dropping seeds on the cleared land. By July, new growth is evident in the fields. By the second year, blueberries blossom and set tiny, sweet, deliciously fragrant fruits. This is the fruit that shouldn't be missed.

Raspberry Buckle

☆ ☆ ☆ ☆ ☆ ☆ ☆ ☆ ☆ ☆ ☆ ☆ ☆ ☆ ☆ ☆ ☆ ☆

Cake

6 cups raspberries
½ cup sugar
1 tablespoon lemon juice
¼ cup butter, at room
    temperature
1 cup sugar
1 cup plain yogurt
3 eggs, lightly beaten
½ cup milk
1 teaspoon almond extract
2 cups unbleached
    all-purpose flour
2 teaspoons baking powder
2 teaspoons baking soda
⅛ teaspoon nutmeg

Topping

¼ cup butter, melted
1 cup unbleached
    all-purpose flour
½ cup firmly packed brown
    sugar
½ teaspoon cinnamon

Here's another variation on the theme. The fruit is covered by a cake layer, which has a tendency to buckle and crack as it bakes. No problem, the crumb topping hides all, while the cake layer becomes permeated with the flavor of raspberries. This is a casual sort of cake, good to serve at brunch or whenever you might serve a coffee cake.

☆ ☆ ☆

Preheat the oven to 350° F. Grease a 9-inch by 13-inch dish and set aside.

Combine the raspberries, ½ cup sugar, and lemon juice in a saucepan. Heat until the sugar dissolves. Spoon into the bottom of the baking dish.

Beat together the butter and 1 cup sugar until light and creamy. Beat in the yogurt, eggs, milk, and almond extract until just combined.

In a separate bowl, sift together the flour, baking powder, baking soda, and nutmeg. Beat into the butter mixture. Pour over the raspberries.

Make the topping by combining the melted butter, 1 cup flour, brown sugar, and cinnamon. Sprinkle on top. Bake in the preheated oven for 1 hour, or until a tester inserted into the cake layer comes out clean.

Serve warm or cooled directly out of the pan.

YIELD: 10 TO 12 SERVINGS

Why, there hasn't been time for the bushes to grow.
That's always the way with the blueberries, though:
There may not have been the ghost of a sign
Of them anywhere under the shade of the pine,
But get the pine out of the way, you may burn
The pasture all over until not a fern
Or grass-blade is left, not to mention a stick,
And presto, they're up all around you as thick
And hard to explain as a conjuror's trick.

It must be on charcoal they fatten their fruit
I taste in them sometimes the flavour of soot.
And after all really they're ebony skinned:
The blue's but a mist from the breath of the wind,
A tarnish that goes at the touch of the hand,
And less than the tan with which pickers are tanned.

Excerpt from "Blueberries" by Robert Frost
(*Collected Poems*, Henry Holt & Company, 1939).

Baked Apples

☆☆☆☆☆☆☆☆☆☆☆☆☆☆☆☆

6 large Rome Beauty or other baking apples
2 tablespoons dried currants
2 tablespoons golden raisins
2 tablespoons toasted slivered almonds (optional)
¼ cup firmly packed light brown sugar
1 tablespoon lemon zest
1 teaspoon cinnamon
½ teaspoon nutmeg
6 teaspoons butter or margarine, cut into pieces
1½ cups hot apple juice
2 teaspoons white sugar

Consider this a crustless apple pie—very easy to make.

☆ ☆ ☆

Preheat the oven to 375° F.

Core the apples to ½ inch from the bottom. Remove a 1-inch strip of skin around the top of each apple. Stand the apples upright in a shallow baking dish that will hold the apples compactly.

Mix together the currants, raisins, almonds, brown sugar, and lemon zest. Fill the centers evenly with the mixture. Sprinkle with cinnamon and nutmeg. Dot with butter. Pour the hot apple juice around apples to a depth of ½ inch.

Bake for 45 to 60 minutes, basting frequently, until the apples are tender when pierced with a fork. Sprinkle the remaining 2 teaspoons of sugar over the apples during the last 5 minutes of baking. (The baking time will depend upon the variety and size of the apple.)

Serve in dessert dishes; spoon the juices remaining in the dish over the apples. Serve warm or at room temperature with cream.

Note: For variation, the raisins and currants can be plumped in apple brandy or sherry for several hours before you fill the apples.

YIELD: 6 SERVINGS

Take nice, large juicy apples, wash and core them well; fill each place that you have cored with brown sugar, cinnamon, raisins, and put a clove in each apple; lay them in a deep dish, pour a teacupful of water in the dish, and put a little sugar on top of each apple; when well done the apples will be broken, then remove them carefully to the dish they are to be served in and pour the syrup over them. To be eaten cold. If you wish them extra nice, glaze them with the beaten whites of three eggs and a half cupful of pulverized sugar and served with whipped cream. I forgot to mention that after the apples are glazed, you must return them to the oven for a few minutes.

"Aunt Babette's" Cook Book (Cincinnati and Chicago: The Bloch Publishing and Printing Co., 1891).

Apple Charlotte

☆☆☆☆☆☆☆☆☆☆☆☆☆☆☆☆☆☆

Filling

3 tablespoons butter or
   margarine
3½ to 4 pounds tart apples,
   peeled, cored, and sliced
   ¼ inch thick (about 8
   cups sliced)
2 tablespoons water
¾ to 1 cup firmly packed
   light brown sugar
1 tablespoon lemon zest
2 tablespoons lemon juice
2 teaspoons cinnamon
¼ teaspoon nutmeg
12 to 14 slices firm white
   bread, crusts removed,
   thinly sliced
½ cup melted butter

Rum Apricot Sauce

1 cup apricot jam
1 tablespoon water
3 tablespoons dark rum

This dessert, something of a fancy variation on Apple Brown Betty, has French origins. The dessert was supposedly named after one Charlotte Buff, on whom Johann Wolfgang von Goethe based the heroine of *Die Leiden des Jungens Werthers,* a very popular novel in its day (1774). The first recipe for Apple Charlotte might be the one that appeared in *American Domestic Cookery* by Maria Eliza Rundell, in 1823.

Lightly grease a 2-quart charlotte mold, soufflé dish, or straight-sided glass baking dish.

In a large skillet, melt the 3 tablespoons butter. Add the apples and water, and cook, covered, over moderate heat, stirring occasionally, until the liquid just begins to boil. Stir in ¾ cup of the brown sugar, the lemon zest, and lemon juice. Cook, uncovered, until the apples are softened and the mixture is thick. All the liquid should be absorbed. Mix in the cinnamon and nutmeg. Taste and add more sugar if needed. Set aside.

Preheat the oven to 375° F.

Cut 3 or more slices of bread into pie shapes to fit the bottom of the mold. The points should meet in the center and fan out like the spokes of a wheel. Brush both sides of the bread with the melted butter and arrange in bottom of mold. Cut 6 or more slices of the remaining bread in half lengthwise. Brush both sides of each rectangle with butter; line the sides of the mold with bread, standing the slices upright and overlapping them slightly. Fill with the well-drained apple mixture. Brush the remaining bread with butter and trim to fit over top of apples. Tap the mold on the work surface and gently press the bread down. Trim excess bread from around the edge until it is flush with the top of the apple charlotte.

Bake for 30 minutes, press the apples down, and bake for 15 minutes longer, or until the top is golden brown. Trim the bread again from around the top edge, if necessary. Let cool on a rack for 15 minutes while you prepare the Rum Apricot Sauce.

In a small saucepan, combine the apricot jam and water. Stir over low heat until the jam is melted. Simmer, stirring occasionally, for 3 minutes. Remove from the heat; strain and blend in the rum. Let cool slightly.

Carefully loosen the charlotte by running a knife around the inside of mold. Invert it onto a serving dish and brush with warm Rum Apricot Sauce. Pour some of the sauce around the base of the charlotte. Serve warm with whipped cream.

YIELD: 8 TO 10 SERVINGS

Berry Fool

☆☆☆☆☆☆☆☆☆☆☆☆

2 cups sliced fresh or frozen strawberries, whole raspberries, or gooseberries
¼ cup sugar
3 tablespoons water
2 teaspoons lemon juice
1 cup heavy whipping cream
1 tablespoon kirsch, fraise des bois, or cherry brandy
Garnish: ⅓ cup toasted macaroon crumbs

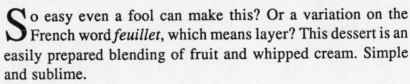

So easy even a fool can make this? Or a variation on the French word *feuillet*, which means layer? This dessert is an easily prepared blending of fruit and whipped cream. Simple and sublime.

☆ ☆ ☆

In a small saucepan, combine the berries, sugar, and water. Bring to a boil, then reduce the heat and simmer for 4 to 5 minutes, or until the juices become syrupy. Pour into a bowl, cover, and refrigerate for 2 hours, or until the berries are very cold. Puree with the lemon juice in a food processor or blender. If you are using raspberries, press the berries through a sieve, collecting as much pulp and juice as possible and discarding the seeds.

Whip the cream until soft peaks form, then add the liqueur or brandy and beat until stiff. Fold the cream into the berry puree. Spoon into 6 dessert dishes or a 1-quart serving dish. Sprinkle with the macaroon crumbs. Serve immediately or cover with plastic and chill for several hours.

Note: If you are using frozen sweetened fruit, defrost and reserve the juice. Heat the juice to boiling, then cook it until the syrup is reduced to 3 tablespoons. Use the reduced juice in place of the water, and eliminate the sugar.

YIELD: 6 SERVINGS

NIAGARA LEAP BY THE WONDERFUL BUISLAY FAMILY.

Raspberry Trifle

☆☆☆☆☆☆☆☆☆☆☆☆☆☆☆☆☆☆

Custard

4 egg yolks
¼ cup sugar
1½ tablespoons cornstarch
Pinch salt
2½ cups milk
2 tablespoons brandy
1 cup heavy whipping cream

Cake and Fruit

12-ounce pound cake or
sponge cake
½ cup raspberry jam
½ to ⅔ cup cream sherry
2 (10-ounce) packages frozen
raspberries, thawed and
drained, or 2 cups fresh,
sweetened with sugar to
taste, and drained

Garnish

1 cup heavy whipping cream
2 tablespoons sifted
confectioners' sugar
¼ teaspoon almond extract
½ cup toasted slivered
almonds
¼ cup fresh raspberries

Did this taste any better when it was known as Tipsy Parson? This English dessert is a favorite no matter where it is served, no matter what it is called.

To make the custard, whisk together the egg yolks, sugar, cornstarch, and salt in a heavy-bottom saucepan until smooth. Add the milk gradually, stirring to remove any lumps. Cook over moderate heat, stirring constantly until the mixture is slightly thickened. Do not let it boil. Remove from the heat; add 1 tablespoon of the brandy. Cover the surface of the pudding with plastic wrap and chill.

Whip the cream until stiff; stir in the remaining 1 tablespoon of brandy. Fold into the chilled custard.

Cut the cake into ¼-inch slices (18 to 20 slices). Spread a layer of jam on half the cake slices, then sandwich the slices together. Using a pastry brush, soak both sides of the cake sandwiches with sherry, then cut them into 4 equal pieces. Arrange half of them over the bottom and part way up sides of the bowl. Spoon on half of the berries. Spread half of the custard over berries. Repeat the layers with the remaining cake pieces, berries, and custard. Cover with plastic wrap and chill for several hours or for up to 2 days.

Before serving, whip the remaining cup of cream until soft peaks form. Add the confectioners' sugar and almond extract and beat until stiff. Pipe whipped cream on top of the trifle. Sprinkle toasted almonds over the top and garnish with fresh raspberries. Serve in dessert dishes.

YIELD: 16 SERVINGS

Puddings

☆☆☆☆☆☆☆☆☆☆☆☆☆☆☆☆☆☆☆☆☆☆☆☆☆

Baked Custard

☆☆☆☆☆☆☆☆☆☆☆☆☆☆☆☆

4 eggs
6 tablespoons sugar
¼ teaspoon salt
3 cups hot milk
1 teaspoon vanilla extract
Freshly grated nutmeg

This is the ultimate in comfort food: soft, smooth, easy to digest, and just like Mom's. Baked custard certainly didn't originate in America, but it has been enjoyed here as much as it has in the Old World.

☆ ☆ ☆

Preheat the oven to 325° F.

In a bowl, lightly beat the eggs with a whisk. Stir in the sugar and salt. Add the hot milk gradually, stirring constantly. Add the vanilla. Strain.

Pour the filling into 6 custard cups or a 1-quart baking dish. Set the cups or baking dish into a shallow pan at least 2 inches deep. Sprinkle the custards with nutmeg. Pour 1 inch of hot water around the custard cups or baking dish.

Bake individual custards for 45 to 50 minutes; bake the large baking dish for 1 to 1¼ hours. The custard is done when a knife inserted 1 inch from the outer edge comes out clean. The center will still be soft.

Remove the custards from the hot water and place in 1 inch of cool water to stop the cooking process. Serve chilled or at room temperature. Custard is delicious served with maple syrup or fresh fruit.

YIELD: 6 SERVINGS

Chocolate Pudding

☆ ☆

Pudding

2 ounces unsweetened
    chocolate
2 ounces semi-sweet
    chocolate or ⅓ cup semi-
    sweet chocolate chips
2 cups milk
½ cup sugar
⅛ teaspoon salt
2 tablespoons cornstarch
2 egg yolks, lightly beaten
1 tablespoon butter, at room
    temperature
1 teaspoon vanilla extract

Topping

1 cup heavy whipping cream
2 tablespoons sifted
    confectioners' sugar
1 tablespoon dark rum

American cooks have always been enamored with kitchen gadgets. When cornstarch manufacturers started giving away pudding molds in the nineteenth century, cornstarch sales soared and cornstarch puddings became very popular. Americans are also enamored with convenience foods. Ever since Jell-o started manufacturing their pudding mix, few children have had the opportunity to taste creamy, flavorful, made-from-scratch cornstarch puddings, like this one.

In a heavy-bottomed saucepan over very low heat, melt the chocolates. Stir in 1¾ cups of the milk, the sugar, and salt. Heat almost to boiling, stirring frequently. Flecks of chocolate will remain until the pudding has finished cooking.

In a small bowl, combine the cornstarch with the remaining ¼ cup milk. Add it to the hot chocolate mixture. Cook over medium heat, stirring until the mixture thickens and comes to a boil. Reduce the heat slightly and boil gently for 1 minute. Remove from the heat.

Gradually stir a few teaspoons of the pudding mixture into the beaten egg yolks, mixing constantly until blended. Continue adding the pudding gradually, until you have added about ½ cup. Pour the yolk mixture back into the pan, stirring until combined. Cook over low heat, stirring constantly, for 2 minutes, until thick and smooth. Remove from the heat.

Stir in small bits of butter at a time and the vanilla, mixing until the butter is melted. Immediately pour into 6 dessert dishes and cover the surface of the puddings with plastic wrap to prevent a skin from forming. Cool on a rack, then chill in the refrigerator.

Just before serving, beat the whipping cream until soft peaks form. Add the confectioners' sugar and rum and beat until stiff. Pipe a portion of whipped cream on top of each pudding.

YIELD: 6 SERVINGS

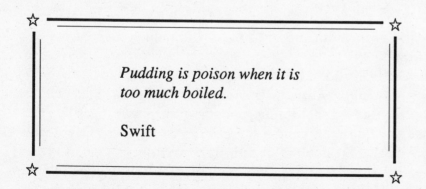

Pudding is poison when it is too much boiled.

Swift

Butterscotch Pudding

☆☆☆☆☆☆☆☆☆☆☆☆☆☆☆☆☆☆☆☆☆☆☆

Pudding

½ cup white sugar
⅓ cup water
2½ cups milk
3 tablespoons butter
¾ cup firmly packed dark
    brown sugar
2 tablespoons all-purpose
    unbleached flour
3 tablespoons cornstarch
⅛ teaspoon salt
4 egg yolks, lightly beaten
1 teaspoon vanilla extract

Topping

1 cup heavy whipping cream
2 tablespoons sifted
    confectioners' sugar
¼ teaspoon nutmeg

Butterscotch is a rich flavor derived from butter, brown sugar, and lemon juice. It should come as no surprise that it was first made in Scotland. Butterscotch has been a favorite for puddings, candies, and dessert sauces ever since it was introduced in the nineteenth century.

☆☆☆

Pour the white sugar into a small heavy-bottomed saucepan or skillet and cook over medium heat without stirring until the sugar melts and is golden brown. Remove from the heat; slowly and carefully pour in the water. (The water will steam and boil up as it hits caramelized sugar.) Cook without stirring until the sugar dissolves. Add 2 cups of the milk and heat almost to boiling. Remove from the heat and stir in the butter. Set aside.

In another heavy-bottomed saucepan, combine the brown sugar, flour, cornstarch, and salt. Add the remaining ½ cup of cold milk gradually, stirring it in with a wire whisk to remove any lumps. Slowly add the hot caramel milk mixture. Cook over medium heat, stirring until the mixture thickens and comes to a boil. Continue stirring and boil for 1 minute. Remove from the heat.

Gradually stir a few teaspoons of the pudding mixture into the beaten egg yolks, mixing constantly until blended. When you have added about ½ cup, pour the yolk mixture back into the pan, stirring until combined. Cook, stirring constantly, for 2 minutes, until thick and smooth. Remove from the heat. Add the vanilla.

Pour into 6 dessert dishes. Cool on a rack, then chill in the refrigerator. Just before serving, beat the whipping cream until stiff and add the confectioners' sugar and nutmeg. Pipe the whipped cream on top of each serving.

YIELD: 6 SERVINGS

The very word pudding has inspired wits and pundits through-out the ages. Pudding doesn't always mean, well, pudding. If someone tells you, "Not a word of pudding!" then say nothing about it (late seventeenth century, early eighteenth century). "I beg your pudding!" means I beg your pardon! (circa 1890). The pudding-club refers to pregnancy (as in "Join the Pudding Club!", twentieth century). A pudding-sleeves is a clergyman (eighteenth to nineteenth century), a piece of pudding is a piece of good luck (c. 1870). Shakespeare seemed to have been quite inspired by pudding, having one character threaten, "I'll let out your puddings," meaning "I will spill your guts." And another time, "He'll yield the crow a pudding one of these days," which is a rather colorful way to talk about death.

Rice Pudding

☆☆☆☆☆☆☆☆☆☆☆☆☆

2 egg yolks
½ cup sugar
2 teaspoons cornstarch
⅛ teaspoon salt
½ teaspoon cinnamon
¼ teaspoon nutmeg
2½ cups warm milk
1 teaspoon vanilla extract
1½ cups cooked long-grain rice
½ cup raisins
Garnish: Freshly grated nutmeg

It has always been a mystery why the best-tasting rice puddings are served at diners, particularly Greek-run diners on the East Coast. But then again, diners often serve the best pies, too. What it comes down to is this: If you want good, old-fashioned desserts, a good old-fashioned diner is often as good as grandmother's.

☆ ☆ ☆

Preheat the oven to 325° F. Lightly grease a 1½-quart baking dish. Set it into a slightly larger pan that is at least 2 inches deep.

In a bowl, whisk together the egg yolks, sugar, cornstarch, salt, cinnamon, nutmeg, and a few tablespoons of the milk; whisk until blended. Add the remaining milk gradually, along with the vanilla. Fold in the rice and raisins.

Spoon the pudding into the baking dish. Pour 1 inch of hot water around the dish. Bake uncovered for 1½ hours, stirring with a fork every 15 minutes during the first hour. This will prevent the rice from settling and will keep the custard creamy. Do not stir during the last half hour. The pudding will be done when the rice looks creamy and almost all of the milk is absorbed.

Remove from water bath and let cool on a rack. Sprinkle with nutmeg. Serve warm or cold with milk, cream, or a fresh fruit sauce.

Note: The raisins can be plumped in sherry for several hours for extra flavor. Drain before using.

YIELD: 6 TO 8 SERVINGS

Little Boy's Pudding

One tea-cup of rice
One tea-cup of sugar
One half tea-cup of butter
One quart of milk
Nutmeg, cinnamon, and salt to taste

Put the butter in melted, and mix all in a pudding dish, and bake it
two hours, stirring frequently, until the rice is swollen.
This is good made without butter.

From *Miss Beecher's Domestic Receipt-Book* by Catherine Esther
Beecher (sister of author Harriet Beecher Stowe) (New York:
Harper and Bros., 1868).

Bread Pudding

☆☆☆☆☆☆☆☆☆☆☆☆☆☆☆☆

4 slices firm white bread
1 to 2 tablespoons soft butter
   or margarine
½ cup raisins
2 eggs
⅓ cup firmly packed light
   brown sugar
Pinch salt
½ teaspoon cinnamon
⅛ teaspoon nutmeg
2¼ cups warm milk
1 teaspoon vanilla extract
1 teaspoon white sugar

A boon to the thrifty housewife . . .

☆ ☆ ☆

Thoroughly grease an 8-inch square or round baking pan.

Toast the bread on both sides until lightly colored. The bread should remain soft inside. Spread butter on both sides of each slice, then cut it up into 1-inch cubes. You should have 2½ to 3 cups of bread cubes. Arrange the bread cubes in the baking pan; sprinkle with raisins.

In a bowl, lightly beat the eggs with a whisk. Add the brown sugar, salt, cinnamon, and nutmeg. Gradually add the warm milk and vanilla, stirring until combined. Pour the mixture over the bread cubes. Let stand for 30 minutes, pressing the bread down occasionally to absorb the custard. Sprinkle the 1 teaspoon of sugar over the top.

Preheat the oven to 325° F. Bake the pudding for 50 to 60 minutes, or until a knife inserted between the center and edge of pan comes out clean. The pudding should be golden brown and puffed.

Cool on a rack. Serve warm or cold with whipped cream and fresh berries.

YIELD: 6 SERVINGS

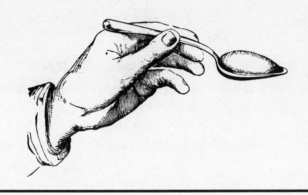

What's the matter with Mary Jane?
She's perfectly well and she hasn't a pain
And it's lovely rice pudding for dinner again!

A. A. Milne

Indian Pudding

☆ ☆ ☆ ☆ ☆ ☆ ☆ ☆ ☆ ☆ ☆ ☆ ☆ ☆ ☆

4 cups milk
⅓ cup yellow cornmeal
¼ cup sugar
¼ teaspoon salt
½ teaspoon cinnamon
½ teaspoon ground ginger
¼ teaspoon nutmeg
2 tablespoons butter
½ cup dark molasses
1 cup light cream

This is one of the very oldest American desserts, taught to the colonists by the natives, who called this dish sagamite. This version tastes faintly reminiscent of pumpkin pie, with its soft creamy texture under a glossy chestnut brown skin. The pudding will be soft when it comes out of the oven, but will firm up when chilled.

☆ ☆ ☆

Lightly grease a 1½-quart baking dish. Set it into a slightly larger pan that is at least 2 inches deep.

In a heavy-bottomed saucepan, heat 3 cups of the milk just to the boiling point. Mix the cornmeal with the remaining cup of cold milk. With a whisk, stir it gradually into the hot milk. Cook over moderate heat for 20 minutes, stirring frequently. The mixture will be slightly thickened. Remove from the heat.

Preheat the oven to 300° F.

Combine the sugar with the salt, cinnamon, ginger, and nutmeg. Add to cornmeal mixture, along with the butter and molasses, stirring until blended.

Pour the pudding into the baking dish. Pour 1 inch of hot water around dish. Place on an oven rack. Carefully spoon the light cream over the top of the pudding; do not stir it in. The cream will form a skin while baking. Bake for 3 hours.

Remove from the oven and place the baking dish on a rack for 15 minutes to allow the pudding to set. Serve warm with vanilla ice cream.

YIELD: 6 SERVINGS

Boiled Indian Pudding

Mix one quart of corn meal, with three quarts of milk; take care it be not lumpy—add three eggs and a gill of molasses; it must be put on at sun rise, to eat at three o' clock; the great art in this pudding is tying the bag properly, as the meal swells, very much.

Persimmon Pudding

☆☆☆☆☆☆☆☆☆☆☆☆☆☆☆☆☆☆☆☆☆

Pudding

1½ cups pureed ripe
    persimmons (3 to 4 large)
1½ teaspoons lemon juice
1½ cups sifted all-purpose
    unbleached flour
1 teaspoon baking powder
1 teaspoon baking soda
½ teaspoon salt
1½ teaspoons cinnamon
1 teaspoon ground ginger
½ teaspoon nutmeg
2 eggs
½ cup granulated sugar
½ cup lightly packed dark
    brown sugar
3 tablespoons melted butter
    or margarine
1 teaspoon vanilla extract
¾ cup milk or half-and-half
½ cup raisins
½ cup chopped walnuts

Hard Sauce

¼ cup butter or margarine, at
    room temperature
1¼ cups sifted confectioners
    sugar
1 teaspoon lemon juice
1 to 2 tablespoons brandy
Nutmeg

Alas, you will have to go to Southern Indiana to taste this pudding made with the authentic American persimmon, a small oval fruit that is a burnt sienna in color. (Indianans describe the color as persimmon color and say there are no other words to describe it.) The persimmons you will find in the supermarket are a Japanese variety that grows well on the West Coast. These fruits are larger, less intensely flavored. Made with either variety, this pudding summons up memories of plum pudding. It looks like a rich, dark chocolate pudding with a chewy crust, but tastes light, fruity, and spicy.

☆ ☆ ☆

To prepare the persimmon puree, cut the fruit in half and scoop out the pulp with a spoon. Discard the skin, stem, and seeds. Puree the pulp in a blender or food processor, or strain through a food mill. Measure out 1½ cups and mix with the lemon juice. Set aside.

Preheat the oven to 350° F. Thoroughly grease and flour a 9-inch square pan.

Sift the flour, baking powder, baking soda, salt, cinnamon, ginger, and nutmeg. Set aside.

Beat the eggs until light. Beat in the sugars, persimmon puree, melted butter, and vanilla. Add the dry ingredients alternately with the milk, mixing just until the batter is smooth and blended. Fold in the raisins and nuts. Spoon into the prepared pan.

Bake for 60 to 70 minutes, or until the pudding pulls away from the sides of the pan, and a pick inserted 1 inch from the edge comes out clean. The center will be a little bit soft. Let cool on a rack for 5 minutes. Cut into squares and serve with chilled hard sauce or whipped cream flavored with a tablespoon of brandy.

Hard Sauce

In a small bowl, beat the butter until creamy. Gradually add the confectioners sugar. Add the lemon juice and 1 tablespoon of the brandy and mix until thoroughly blended and fluffy. Add more brandy if desired. Spoon the sauce into a sauce dish and sprinkle with nutmeg. Chill before using. Serve over the hot pudding.

YIELD: 6 TO 8 SERVINGS

What a time the early colonists must have had tasting the new foods they encountered! Take persimmons, which are plentiful in the Midwest and the Carolinas. The taste of a ripe persimmon is said to be something like a cross between a guava, mango, apricot, and tomato—very tasty in puddings and cakes. But the unripe persimmon is so acidic, it could, as one early diarist recorded, "drawe a man's mouth awrie with much torment." One must pity the poor explorer who had not yet learned the difference between the ripe and unripe fruit.

Chocolate Mousse

☆ ☆ ☆ ☆ ☆ ☆ ☆ ☆ ☆ ☆ ☆ ☆ ☆ ☆ ☆ ☆ ☆ ☆ ☆

4 ounces semi-sweet
  chocolate or ⅔ cup semi-
  sweet chocolate chips
2 ounces unsweetened
  chocolate
¼ cup strong coffee
¼ cup sugar
4 egg yolks
4 egg whites, at room
  temperature
Pinch salt
3 tablespoons sugar
1 cup heavy whipping cream
1 tablespoon brandy or 1
  teaspoon vanilla extract

Mousses originated in France but have become quite popular here since the 1960s. This mousse has intense chocolate flavor.

☆ ☆ ☆

In a heavy-bottomed saucepan over very low heat, melt the chocolates. Stir in the coffee and ¼ cup sugar. Transfer the mixture to a bowl and set aside to cool.

Add the egg yolks to the cooled chocolate mixture, one at a time, beating well after each addition.

In the bowl of an electric mixer, beat the egg whites until foamy. Add the salt and beat until stiff but not dry. Sprinkle in the remaining 3 tablespoons of sugar, 1 tablespoon at a time, beating well after each addition. Mix a quarter of the beaten egg whites into the chocolate mixture, just enough to lighten it. Gently fold in the remaining egg whites.

Beat the whipping cream until stiff. Beat in the brandy or vanilla; then gently fold into the chocolate mixture.

Spoon into 6 soufflé or dessert dishes. Serve chilled with additional whipped cream and a sprinkling of chocolate shavings if desired.

YIELD: 6 SERVINGS

Uncle Sam says:

Growing children need plenty of milk . . . daily

It's a treat for children to eat milk with a spoon . . . just make it into delicious

RENNET-CUSTARDS

"JUNKET" is the trademark of Chr. Hansen's Laboratory, Inc., for its rennet and other food products, and is registered in the United States and Canada.

One of the best ways to increase the milk consumption of growing children — and adults too — is to make it into delicious rennet-custards.

For rennet-custards provide the calcium, valuable proteins and vitamins of milk in a readily digestible form due to the rennet enzyme — and above all, everyone loves to eat them. And milk is "Nature's most nearly perfect food" . . . a nutrition essential.

Make rennet-custards with either:

"JUNKET" RENNET POWDER — 6 tempting flavors. *Needs no sugar.* At all grocers.

"JUNKET" RENNET TABLETS — Not sweetened. Add sugar, flavor to taste. Economical. At grocers and druggists.

Send for FREE Recipe Book

Over 100 recipes for bright, colorful desserts and ice creams. Write "The 'Junket' Folks," Chr. Hansen's Laboratory, Inc., Dept. 302, Little Falls, N. Y.

Lemon Mousse

☆☆☆☆☆☆☆☆☆☆☆☆☆☆☆

2 teaspoons unflavored
    gelatin
3 tablespoons cold water
3 egg yolks
½ cup sugar
1 tablespoon lemon zest
⅔ cup lemon juice
3 egg whites, at room
    temperature
⅛ teaspoon cream of tartar
Pinch salt
¼ cup sugar
1 cup heavy whipping cream
Garnish: Thin slices of lemon

In a small bowl, sprinkle the gelatin over the cold water. Stir and set aside to soften.

In the top part of a double boiler, beat the egg yolks with a wire whisk until thick and lemon colored. Gradually add the ½ cup sugar, beating until thoroughly blended. Mix in the lemon zest and lemon juice. Place the pan over simmering water. The water should not touch the bottom of the pan. Cook, stirring constantly, until the mixture lightly coats a metal spoon. Add the softened gelatin, stirring until dissolved.

Remove from the heat. Refrigerate or place the pan in a bowl of ice water, stirring until the mixture mounds slightly when dropped from a spoon. It should be cold but not set.

Beat the egg whites until foamy. Add the cream of tartar and salt, and beat until soft peaks form. Gradually add the remaining ¼ cup sugar and continue beating until stiff but not dry. Gently fold into the mousse mixture. Whip the cream until stiff. Fold half of it into the mousse.

Spoon into a 1½-quart soufflé dish or 8 custard cups or dessert dishes. Chill until firm. Pipe dollops of the remaining whipped cream on top of each portion. Garnish with thin slices of lemon.

YIELD: 8 SERVINGS

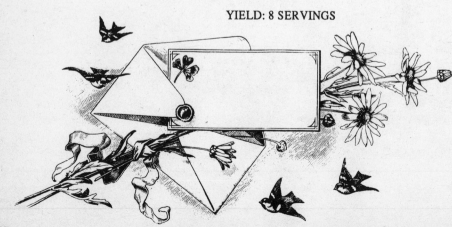

Cookies

☆☆☆☆☆☆☆☆☆☆☆☆☆☆☆☆☆☆☆☆☆☆☆☆

Chocolate Chip Cookies

☆ ☆

2¼ cups sifted all-purpose flour
1 teaspoon salt
1 cup butter
¾ cup firmly packed brown sugar
¾ cup white sugar
2 eggs, beaten
1 teaspoon baking soda
1 teaspoon hot water
1 cup chopped nuts
12 ounces (2 cups) semi-sweet chocolate chips
1 teaspoon vanilla extract

There was a time, not so long ago, when chocolate came in great slabs; there were no chips, bits, and morsels. In 1933, Mrs. Ruth Wakefield was making a batch of butter dewdrop cookies (or butter drop-do's; accounts vary) for the guests at the Tollhouse Inn and she was in a rush. Instead of melting the chocolate as her recipe required, she decided to chop up the chocolate and let it melt into the cookies as they baked. The chocolate bits retained their shape, and the chocolate chip cookie was born. At first Mrs. Wakefield called the cookies "chocolate crunch cookies" (or chocolate crispies, again depending on who you read), but soon changed the name to Toll House Cookies. Before long, the recipe was published in a newspaper and sales of Nestle's Chocolate began to rise. Recognizing a good thing when they saw it on the sales charts, Nestle's began printing the recipe, with Mrs. Wakefield's permission, on packages of specially scored chocolate bars that easily broke into bits. A few years later, Nestle's bought the legal rights to use the Toll House trade name and began marketing chocolate chips.

☆ ☆ ☆

Preheat the oven to 375° F. Lightly grease 2 cookie sheets.

Sift together the flour and salt. Set aside.

In a mixing bowl, cream together the butter and sugars. Add the eggs. Combine the baking soda and hot water and add to the creamed mixture. Stir in the flour mixture. Then stir in the nuts, chocolate chips, and vanilla.

Drop the dough by the teaspoon onto the cookie sheets about 1 inch apart and bake for 8 to 10 minutes. Cool on a wire rack.

YIELD: ABOUT 100 SMALL COOKIES

KING OF THE BORDER MEN!

The Cooky Jar

As soon as school is out at night
All children, near and far,
Go rushing home, in one mad flight,
To find the Cooky jar!
(So keep it filled for their delight;
You know how children are.)

Anon.

Oatmeal Cookies

☆ ☆ ☆ ☆ ☆ ☆ ☆ ☆ ☆ ☆ ☆ ☆ ☆ ☆ ☆ ☆ ☆ ☆ ☆ ☆

1½ cups all-purpose
    unbleached flour
1 teaspoon baking soda
1 teaspoon cinnamon
½ teaspoon salt
1 cup butter or margarine,
    at room temperature
1 cup firmly packed dark
    brown sugar
½ cup white sugar
2 eggs
2 tablespoons molasses
¼ cup hot water
1 teaspoon vanilla extract
3 cups rolled oats (not
    instant)
1½ cups raisins
1 cup chopped walnuts
    (optional)

These are satisfying, homey cookies—studded with raisins and nuts. A bite conjures up images of "Leave-it-to-Beaver" moms and after-school snacks of cookies and milk.

Preheat the oven to 375° F.

Sift together the flour, baking soda, cinnamon, and salt. Set aside.

In a large mixing bowl, beat together the butter and sugars until creamy. Add the eggs, one at a time, beating well after each addition. Mix in the molasses, hot water, and vanilla, beating until fluffy. Stir in the dry ingredients, blending thoroughly. Add the rolled oats, raisins, and walnuts, stirring until combined.

Place rounded tablespoons of the mixture 2 inches apart on ungreased cookie sheets. Press with a wet spoon or spatula to flatten.

Bake for 12 to 15 minutes or until golden. Let the cookies cool on the cookie sheets for a few minutes. Then use a spatula to carefully remove them to wire racks to cool completely.

YIELD: 5 DOZEN COOKIES

Cookies, Cup-Cakes, Doughnuts

Oh, weary mothers, rolling dough
Don't you wish that food would grow?
How happy all the world would be,
With a cookie bush, and a doughnut tree.

Mrs. Harold J. Wells (from *The 20th Century Bride's Cook Book*, 1929).

Peanut Butter Cookies

☆ ☆ ☆ ☆ ☆ ☆ ☆ ☆ ☆ ☆ ☆ ☆ ☆ ☆ ☆ ☆ ☆ ☆ ☆ ☆

1¾ cups all-purpose
   unbleached flour
½ teaspoon baking powder
½ teaspoon baking soda
½ teaspoon salt
½ cup butter or margarine, at
   room temperature
½ cup crunchy peanut butter
½ cup firmly packed dark
   brown sugar
½ cup white sugar
1 egg
3 tablespoons orange juice
1 teaspoon vanilla extract
Garnish: ½ cup chopped
   peanuts

Peanuts are thought to have originated in Brazil and found their way to Europe via the Portuguese explorers. From Europe, peanuts spread throughout the world, making the journey from Africa to America via African slaves. Since the Civil War, peanuts have been an important agricultural crop in the South, where the little ground nut is also known as a ground-pea and a goober.

In 1890, peanut butter was invented by a St. Louis doctor who promoted it as a health food. It was an instant hit in the U.S. Meanwhile, to the rest of the world, peanuts are mostly valued as a source of oil and as cattle feed. Their loss!

☆ ☆ ☆

Sift together the flour, baking powder, baking soda, and salt. Set aside.

In a large mixing bowl, beat together the butter, peanut butter, and sugars until creamy. Beat in the egg. Mix in the orange juice and vanilla, beating until fluffy. Stir in the dry ingredients, blending thoroughly. Wrap and chill the dough for 1 hour or until firm.

Preheat the oven to 375° F.

Shape the dough into 1-inch balls. Arrange them 2 inches apart on ungreased cookie sheets. Flatten the balls with a wet fork twice, pressing a criss-cross pattern into each top. Sprinkle with the chopped peanuts.

Bake for 10 to 12 minutes or until golden. Let the cookies cool on the cookie sheets for a few minutes. Then use a spatula to carefully remove them to wire racks to cool completely.

YIELD: 3 DOZEN COOKIES

National Peanut Festival

Some 3 to 4 tons of roasted peanuts are consumed at the National Peanut Festival held in Dothan, Alabama, every October— and that's not counting the peanuts that are eaten in the annual bake-off in the form of cookies, pies, ice cream, and candies. That is counting, however, the peanuts that are dumped from cement trucks at the festival parade.

Don't want to miss the festival this year? For dates and more information, contact: National Peanut Festival Association, 1691 Ross Clark, Circle, S.E., Dothan, Alabama 36301; 205-793-4323.

Snickerdoodles

☆ ☆ ☆ ☆ ☆ ☆ ☆ ☆ ☆ ☆ ☆ ☆ ☆ ☆ ☆ ☆

2¾ cups all-purpose
    unbleached flour
1 teaspoon baking soda
1 teaspoon cream of tartar
½ teaspoon salt
1 cup butter, margarine, or
    shortening, at room
    temperature
1⅓ cups sugar
2 eggs
1 teaspoon vanilla extract
1 tablespoon cinnamon
3 tablespoons sugar

Like many of our cookies, these are probably the invention of German or Pennsylvania Dutch settlers. We're not sure what the name conjures up (it's probably a nonsense word), but snickerdoodles emerge from the oven as round little pillows delicately flavored with a cinnamon and sugar coating.

☆ ☆ ☆

Sift together the flour, baking soda, cream of tartar, and salt. Set aside.

In a large mixing bowl, beat together the butter and the 1⅓ cups sugar until creamy. Add the eggs, one at a time, beating well after each addition. Add the vanilla. Stir in the dry ingredients, blending thoroughly. Wrap and chill the dough for 1 hour.

Preheat the oven to 375° F.

Shape the dough into 1-inch balls. Combine the cinnamon and remaining 3 tablespoons sugar. Roll the balls of dough in the mixture. Arrange them 2 inches apart on ungreased baking sheets.

Bake for 12 minutes or until golden. Remove the cookies to wire racks to cool completely.

YIELD: 5 DOZEN COOKIES

CHAS. L. DAVIS' CELEBRATED ALVIN JOSLIN COMEDY COMPANY.

180 LAUGHS IN 180 MINUTES.

Scotch Shortbread

☆☆☆☆☆☆☆☆☆☆☆☆☆☆☆☆☆☆☆☆☆

1½ cups sifted all-purpose unbleached flour
1 cup sifted confectioners sugar
½ cup cornstarch
¼ teaspoon salt
1 cup butter, cut into small pieces (do not substitute margarine)
1 teaspoon vanilla extract

There's no question of the origin of these buttery morsels. There was a significant wave of Scottish immigration to the South in the early 1700s, and with them came shortbread (short, or shortening, in the form of butter, and bread because these cookies aren't particularly sweet). This recipe makes very buttery, very crisp shortbreads, as close to the traditional old-time Scottish shortbread flavor as possible.

Preheat the oven to 325° F.

In a large mixing bowl, combine the flour, confectioners sugar, cornstarch, and salt. Using your fingers, blend the butter and vanilla into the flour mixture until fully absorbed. Shape the dough into a pancake, then knead or mix well for 10 minutes. (With an electric mixer, beat for 5 minutes.) Place the dough in an ungreased 8-inch or 9-inch square baking pan, a 9-inch round pie plate, or a 9-inch pan with a removable bottom. Flatten the dough into an even layer. If the dough is too sticky to spread, chill it for a few minutes first. With a knife, score the dough part way through and mark into squares or wedges. Prick the surface of the shortbread with a fork.

Bake for 35 to 40 minutes until light golden. Do not overbake. Remove from the oven and cut into squares or wedges while still hot. Cool on a rack before removing from the pan.

YIELD: 36 SQUARES OR 12 WEDGES

172

Shortbreads were so popular they inspired songs, such as this one from Virginia.

Three little children, lying in bed
Two were sick, and the other most dead!
Sent for the doctor, the doctor said:
"Feed these children on short' nin' bread."

Mamma's little baby loves short'nin', short'nin'
Mamma's little baby loves short'nin' bread.
Mamma's little baby loves short'nin', short'nin'
Mamma's little baby loves short'nin' bread!

Brandy Snaps

☆☆☆☆☆☆☆☆☆☆☆☆☆☆☆☆

1 cup all-purpose
  unbleached flour
½ cup sugar
⅛ teaspoon salt
½ teaspoon ground ginger
½ cup light molasses
½ cup butter or margarine
2 tablespoons brandy

B randy snaps are cookies flavored with brandy, ginger, and molasses, close cousins to ginger snaps. They date at least as far back as the Middle Ages, where they were popular items at fairs in England. In particular, brandy snaps are associated with the Nottingham Fair, which was held on the first Thursday in October and was famous as the premiere showcase for geese. People came from all over the English Midlands to select their geese, which were driven there in flocks by gooseherds armed only with crooks to keep the cantankerous geese in line.

☆ ☆ ☆

Preheat the oven to 325° F.

Mix together the flour, sugar, salt, and ginger. Set aside. In a saucepan, heat the molasses just to the boiling point. Stir in the butter. Add the dry ingredients gradually and cook, stirring until hot and blended. Remove from the heat. Add the brandy.

Place the pan over hot water to keep the mixture soft. Drop by the teaspoon 3 inches apart onto ungreased cookie sheets. Allow about 6 cookies to each cookie sheet.

Bake for 7 to 8 minutes, until bubbly and golden. Cool for about 2 minutes, until the cookies will hold together. Using a wide spatula, quickly loosen one cookie at a time and place it on a paper towel or drape it over a rolling pin to cool in a curved shape. If the cookies harden before they are removed from the cookie sheet, reheat in the oven for a minute.

When the cookies are cool, store immediately in an airtight container.

Note: Brandy snaps can be shaped into a cylinder, forming them around a wooden spoon or dowel. The ends then can be dipped into chocolate. Large brandy snaps can be filled with whipped cream or ice cream, piped in with a pastry bag. Serve ice cream-filled brandy snaps with chocolate sauce.

YIELD: 3 DOZEN COOKIES

A Home Favorite

Housewives tell their daughters how much good bread depends on good flour and that there's no surer way to have good bread, cake and pastry than by using GOLD MEDAL FLOUR — always.

WASHBURN-CROSBY CO.

Spritz Cookies

☆☆☆☆☆☆☆☆☆☆☆☆☆☆☆

2¼ cups all-purpose
    unbleached flour
¼ cup cornstarch
½ teaspoon baking powder
¼ teaspoon salt
1 cup butter, at room
    temperature
¾ cup sugar
1 egg or 2 egg yolks
1 teaspoon vanilla extract
½ teaspoon almond extract
Garnish: Colored sugar
    crystals, chocolate
    sprinkles, finely chopped
    nuts, or halved candied
    cherries

Preheat the oven to 375° F.
    Sift together the flour, cornstarch, baking powder, and salt. Set aside.

In a large mixing bowl, beat together the butter and sugar until creamy. Beat in the egg. Mix in the vanilla and almond extracts, beating until fluffy. Stir in the dry ingredients, mixing well.

Pack the dough into a cookie press fitted with a decorative plate. Press the dough onto ungreased cookie sheets, 1 inch apart. Decorate with the assorted garnishes.

Bake for 10 to 12 minutes, or until the edges of the cookies are lightly browned. Remove from the pan and cool on wire racks.

Note: To make **Chocolate Spritz Cookies**, add 2 ounces of melted bittersweet or semi-sweet chocolate to the butter. To make **Spice Spritz**, add ½ teaspoon cinnamon, ¼ teaspoon nutmeg, and ¼ teaspoon ground cloves to the dry ingredients.

YIELD: 4 TO 5 DOZEN

Sand Tarts

☆☆☆☆☆☆☆☆☆☆☆☆☆

2 cups all-purpose flour
1 teaspoon baking powder
¼ teaspoon salt
½ cup butter or margarine,
    at room temperature
1 cup sugar
1 egg
1 egg yolk
1 teaspoon orange zest
1 teaspoon orange or vanilla
    extract
1 egg white
2 teaspoons water
2 tablespoons sugar
½ teaspoon cinnamon
Garnish: ½ cup slivered
    almonds

Sift together the flour, baking powder, and salt. Set aside. In a large mixing bowl, beat together the butter and sugar until creamy. Beat in the egg, egg yolk, orange zest, and orange extract, beating until fluffy. Stir in the dry ingredients, blending thoroughly. Divide the dough in half and wrap each portion in plastic. Refrigerate for 2 hours or until firm enough to handle.

Preheat the oven to 350° F.

Working with one portion of the dough at a time, roll out the dough ⅛ inch thick on a lightly floured board or pastry cloth. Cut the dough into squares or diamond shapes. Carefully lift the cookies with a spatula onto ungreased cookie sheets.

Make an egg wash by combining the egg white with the water. Brush the tops with the egg wash. Combine the remaining 2 tablespoons sugar with the cinnamon and sprinkle on top of the cookies. Garnish with the slivered almonds.

Bake for 8 to 10 minutes or until the edges turn golden. Let the cookies cool on the cookie sheets for a few minutes. Then use a spatula to carefully remove them to wire racks to cool completely.

YIELD: 3 TO 4 DOZEN

Many families have owed their prosperity full as much to the propriety of female management, as to the knowledge and activity of the father.

Mrs. J. S. Bradley's Housekeeper's Guide (Cincinnati: H. M. Rulison, 1853).

Molasses Cookies

☆ ☆ ☆ ☆ ☆ ☆ ☆ ☆ ☆ ☆ ☆ ☆ ☆ ☆ ☆ ☆ ☆ ☆

**2¼ cups all-purpose
  unbleached flour
2 teaspoons baking soda
¼ teaspoon salt
1 teaspoon cinnamon
½ teaspoon ground ginger
¼ teaspoon ground cloves
¼ teaspoon allspice
¾ cup butter or margarine, at
  room temperature
1 cup firmly packed dark
  brown sugar
1 egg
⅓ cup dark molasses
Granulated sugar**

Molasses wasn't exactly the sweetener of choice in early American cooking, it was just about the only affordable sweetener (honey and maple syrup were available in limited quantities, depending on where you lived). In the early days of the republic, molasses played an important role in making slave trading lucrative. Slavers would capture Africans to fill their ships bound for the the West Indies. In the West Indies, the ships would be loaded with barrels of molasses bound for the States, where much of it was distilled into rum. Then they would carry timber and other New World products back to Europe. Abolitionists in New England called for a boycott of molasses and exhorted people to use maple syrup instead. "Make your own sugar," was the advice of the *Farmer's Almanac* in 1803, "and send not to the Indies for it. Feast not on the toil, pain, and misery of the wretched."

Eventually, a growing cane sugar industry in the South, and a growing sugar beet industry, made white sugar affordable, and it replaced molasses in most recipes.

Preheat the oven to 375° F. Lightly grease 2 cookie sheets.

Sift together the flour, baking soda, salt, cinnamon, ginger, cloves, and allspice. Set aside.

In a large mixing bowl, beat together the butter and brown sugar until creamy. Beat in the egg and molasses. Stir in the dry ingredients, blending thoroughly. If the dough is too soft to handle, chill in the refrigerator for 1 hour. Shape the cookie dough into balls the size of walnuts. Dip the tops of each ball into white sugar. Place them, sugar side up, 2 inches apart, on the prepared cookie sheets.

Bake for 10 to 12 minutes, or until lightly browned. Remove from the cookie sheets and cool on wire racks.

YIELD: 4 DOZEN

In another time, another place, molasses cookies were also called Joe Froggers. It seems that in Marblehead, Massachusetts, there lived an old Black gentleman who was known as Uncle Joe. Uncle Joe lived on the edge of a frog pond and enjoyed a certain reputation for making the best cookies in town, as large as lily pads and as dark as the frogs in the pond. Seamen stocked up on Joe Froggers, as they kept well in sea chests, and spread the fame of these cookies when they traded them for rum.

Gingerbread Men

☆☆☆☆☆☆☆☆☆☆☆☆☆☆☆☆☆☆

2½ cups all-purpose
   unbleached flour
½ teaspoon baking soda
¼ teaspoon salt
2 teaspoons ground ginger
½ teaspoon cinnamon
¼ teaspoon allspice
½ cup margarine or
   vegetable shortening, at
   room temperature
½ cup firmly packed light
   brown sugar
½ cup dark molasses
2 tablespoons water
Garnish: Currants or raisins
   and cinnamon candies

Traditionally eaten during Christmastime, these cookies are welcome any time of the year. Legend has it that Queen Elizabeth I of England invented gingerbread men. To bite off their heads?

Sift together the flour, baking soda, salt, ginger, cinnamon, and allspice. Set aside.

In a large mixing bowl, beat the margarine until creamy. Add the brown sugar gradually and beat until fluffy. Stir in the molasses and water. Add the dry ingredients, mixing until well blended. Wrap the dough in plastic and refrigerate until chilled, 1 to 2 hours.

Preheat the oven to 375° F. Lightly grease 2 cookie sheets.

On a lightly floured board or pastry cloth, roll out the dough to a thickness of about ³⁄₁₆ inch. Cut with gingerbread cookie cutters. Carefully lift the cookies with a large spatula and place on the cookie sheets. Decorate with currants or raisins and cinnamon candies

Bake for 8 to 10 minutes, until set. Let the cookies cool on the cookie sheets for a few minutes. Then use a spatula to carefully remove them to wire racks to cool completely.

YIELD: 12 TO 16 GINGERBREAD MEN

The most difficult aspect of rolled cookies is keeping the dough from sticking to the work surface. If too much flour is used, the dough becomes tough. Instead of simply flouring your work surface, try using a mix of equal parts flour and confectioners' sugar.

Hermits

☆ ☆ ☆ ☆ ☆ ☆ ☆ ☆ ☆

1⅓ cups all-purpose unbleached flour
½ teaspoon baking soda
1 teaspoon cinnamon
½ teaspoon nutmeg
¼ teaspoon ground cloves
¼ teaspoon allspice
¼ teaspoon salt
½ cup butter or margarine, at room temperature
1 cup firmly packed dark brown sugar
1 egg
½ cup sour cream
1 teaspoon vanilla extract
1 cup chopped raisins or dried currants
¾ cup chopped walnuts or hickory nuts

Is this a recipe for an authentic hermit? Some would say not—hermits should be bar cookies, studded with raisins or currants—perhaps the ancestor of brownies and blondies. One theory goes that hermits were invented on Cape Cod and packed in the sea chests of trading ships. The cookies kept fresh because they were rich with dried fruits. A good theory, but none other than Miss Fanny Farmer made her hermits as drop cookies back in the 1896 edition of her famous cookbook, and some cookbook writers suggest that hermits are simply a variation on the British cookie known as a jumble. Round or square, these are deliciously moist, chewy cookies, great to pack in sea chests and lunch boxes.

☆ ☆ ☆

Preheat the oven to 350° F. Lightly grease several cookie sheets.

Sift together the flour, baking soda, cinnamon, nutmeg, cloves, allspice, and salt. Set aside.

In a large mixing bowl, beat together the butter and sugar until creamy. Add the egg and beat until fluffy. Mix in the sour cream and vanilla. Stir in the dry ingredients, blending thoroughly. Add the raisins and nuts, stirring until combined. Place rounded teaspoons of the mixture 2 inches apart on the cookie sheets.

Bake for 12 to 15 minutes, or until golden. Remove from the cookie sheets and cool on wire racks.

YIELD: 4 DOZEN

Stupid people may eat, but shouldn't talk. Their mouths will do well enough as banks of deposit but not of issue.

The Household Companion and Family Receipt Book by C. B. Unzicker (Cincinnati: Unzicker Co., 1870).

Sugar Cookies

☆☆☆☆☆☆☆☆☆☆☆☆☆☆☆

2 cups all-purpose
   unbleached flour
1 teaspoon baking powder
½ teaspoon salt
½ cup butter or margarine, at
   room temperature
1 cup sugar
1 egg
1 tablespoon milk
1½ teaspoons vanilla extract
Garnish: Granulated sugar or
   sugar crystals

George Washington probably would be surprised to learn that cherry pies are associated with his name. His own favorite dessert was said to be Martha's "sugar cakes," which she rolled thin and cut rather large. These sugar cookies would probably delight old George.

☆ ☆ ☆

Sift together the flour, baking powder, and salt. Set aside.

Beat together the butter and sugar until creamy. Beat in the egg. Mix in the milk and vanilla, beating until fluffy. Stir in the dry ingredients, blending thoroughly. Divide the dough in half and wrap each portion in plastic. Refrigerate for 2 hours or until firm enough to handle.

Preheat the oven to 375° F. Lightly grease several cookie sheets.

Working with one portion of the dough at a time, roll out the dough ⅛ inch thick on a lightly floured board or pastry cloth. Cut out with a 3-inch round cookie cutter. Carefully lift the cookies with a large spatula onto the prepared cookie sheets. Sprinkle with sugar.

Bake for 8 to 10 minutes, or until the edges are lightly browned. Let the cookies cool on the cookie sheets for a few minutes. Then use a spatula to carefully remove them to wire racks to cool completely.

YIELD: 24 TO 30 COOKIES

Fancy cookie cutters became popular sometime in the 18th century, but they reached a peak of popularity in 1913, when Walter Baker and Co. Ltd. published a recipe for "Turkey Trots," a rolled cookie that required a turkey-shaped cookie cutter. The cookie was named after the ragtime dance craze, which lasted through World War I.

Chocolate Brownies

☆ ☆ ☆ ☆ ☆ ☆ ☆ ☆ ☆ ☆ ☆ ☆ ☆ ☆ ☆ ☆ ☆ ☆

2 ounces unsweetened chocolate
2 ounces semi-sweet chocolate, or ⅓ cup semi-sweet chocolate chips
½ cup butter or margarine
1 cup sugar
¼ teaspoon salt
2 eggs
1 teaspoon vanilla extract
½ cup all-purpose unbleached flour
½ cup chopped walnuts

One often reads about the importance of the Sears, Roebuck catalog to rural America in the nineteenth century, but who would have guessed that the first published brownie recipe appeared in that catalog in 1897?

☆ ☆ ☆

Preheat the oven to 350° F. Lightly grease and flour an 8-inch square baking pan.

In a medium-size heavy-bottomed saucepan, melt the chocolates and butter over low heat, stirring until smooth. Remove from the heat and stir in the sugar and salt. Add the eggs, one at a time, beating well after each addition. Stir in the vanilla, flour, and nuts, mixing until blended. Spoon into the prepared pan.

Bake for about 25 minutes, or until the top feels dry and looks shiny. The inside will be soft, but will firm up when cold. Cool completely in the pan on a rack, then cut into squares.

YIELD: 16 TO 25 BROWNIES

Chocolate Tips

Ever since a certain Dr. James Baker invested in the first chocolate mill in the New World, Americans have conducted a love affair with chocolate, buying Baker brand chocolate to this day for their cakes, brownies, and cookies.

Recently, though, Americans have begun to take note of other high-quality brands, imported and domestic. To determine whether a chocolate is of high quality, look for cocoa butter in the ingredients list. Only the good brands have it; others use less expensive vegetable oils, which extend the shelf life of the chocolate by maintaining the fresh appearance of chocolate, but they don't do much for the flavor.

Chocolate quality is actually determined during the manufacturing process. After they are picked, cocoa beans are fermented; then they are processed to separate the cocoa butter from the rest of the bean. What is left is called chocolate liquor. During the manufacture of chocolate, the cocoa butter (or vegetable oil) is remixed with the chocolate liquor. Sugar may be added to make semi-sweet, bittersweet, or sweet chocolate; milk solids may be added for milk chocolate.

Lecithin may be added along with the cocoa butter to improve the viscosity. It also allows more of the chocolate flavor, which can be masked by pure cocoa butter, to come through.

You can substitute unsweetened cocoa powder for unsweetened chocolate, using 3 tablespoons of cocoa plus 1 tablespoon of vegetable oil for every ounce of chocolate.

Lemon Bars

☆ ☆ ☆ ☆ ☆ ☆ ☆ ☆ ☆ ☆ ☆ ☆ ☆ ☆

Cookie Crust

2 cups all-purpose
   unbleached flour
½ cup confectioners sugar
Pinch salt
1 teaspoon lemon zest
1 cup butter or margarine, at
   room temperature

Lemon Filling

4 eggs
2 cups white sugar
1 tablespoon lemon zest
6 tablespoons lemon juice
2 tablespoons all-purpose
   unbleached flour
1 teaspoon baking powder
Garnish: 2 to 3 tablespoons
   confectioners sugar

This recipe makes a rich, buttery cookie. It is a good idea to place the cut bars on paper towels to absorb some of the excess butter. For variation, consider sprinkling the bars with coconut flakes instead of the powdered sugar.

☆ ☆ ☆

Preheat the oven to 350° F. Lightly grease a 9-inch by 13-inch baking pan.

To make the cookie crust, combine the flour, ½ cup confectioners sugar, and salt. Add the lemon zest and butter, mixing until thoroughly blended. Using the heel of your hand or the back of a spoon, gently spread the mixture over the bottom of pan. Bake for 20 minutes.

While crust is baking, prepare the filling. Beat the eggs until light. Then gradually add the sugar, beating until thick and lemon colored. Add the lemon zest, lemon juice, flour, and baking powder, blending until well combined.

Pour the lemon mixture over the baked warm cookie crust and return the pan to the oven for 20 to 25 minutes, or until the top is a golden brown. The filling should be soft.

Sift the remaining 2 to 3 tablespoons confectioners sugar over the cookies while they are still warm. Cool on a rack for at least 30 minutes before cutting. Cut into squares or bars.

YIELD: ABOUT 35 BARS

Chocolate Meringue Kisses

☆☆☆☆☆☆☆☆☆☆☆☆☆☆☆☆☆☆☆☆☆☆☆☆☆☆☆☆

3 egg whites, at room temperature
⅛ teaspoon cream of tartar
⅛ teaspoon salt
1 cup sugar
3 tablespoons unsweetened cocoa powder
½ teaspoon vanilla extract
6-ounce package semi-sweet chocolate chips
½ cup chopped hazelnuts or walnuts

Old cookbooks might call these "forgotten cookies" because they were baked last as the oven cooled after a session of baking breads or cakes. The baker would put the kisses in the "slack oven" and avoid looking into the oven as they slowly baked, lest more heat was lost. Under those circumstances, the kisses were sometimes forgotten.

Preheat the oven to 250° F. Line 2 cookie sheets with aluminum foil. Lightly grease the foil, then sprinkle with flour to coat completely. Shake out any excess flour.

In the large bowl of an electric mixer, beat the egg whites until foamy, add the cream of tartar and salt and beat until soft peaks form. Gradually sprinkle in the sugar, 1 tablespoon at a time, beating well after each addition. Continue beating until stiff and glossy. Sift the cocoa over the meringue. With a rubber spatula, fold the cocoa into the mixture along with the vanilla, chocolate chips, and nuts. Drop by the teaspoonful onto the prepared cookie sheets. Bring the spoon up through the meringue to shape like Hershey's Kisses.

Bake for 25 to 30 minutes or until crisp. Let the cookies cool on the cookie sheets for a few minutes. Then use a spatula to carefully remove them to wire racks to cool completely. These are best when freshly made, but they will keep for 3 to 4 days in an airtight container.

Note: To remove hazelnut skins, preheat the oven to 300° F. Place the hazelnuts on a cookie sheet and for bake 12 to 15 minutes, stirring occasionally until lightly toasted. Place the nuts in a cloth towel; rub the towel over the nuts to remove the skins.

YIELD: 48 COOKIES

Index

☆ ☆

Pie, Coconut, 92

D

Deep-Dish Peach Pie, 78
Devil's Food Cake, 8
Dumplings, Apple, 126

F

Fool, Berry, 142
Frosting
  Brown Sugar, 62
  Burnt Sugar, 64
  Chocolate, 55
      Glaze, 22-23
  Coconut Pecan, 60
  Cream Cheese, 63
  Fudge, 54
  Glossy Chocolate Glaze, 56
  Orange, 59
  Sea Foam, 61
  Seven Minute, 58
  Vanilla, 57
Fruit desserts
  Apple Brown Betty, 124
  Apple Charlotte, 140-141
  Apple Crisp, 120
  Apple Dumplings, 126
  Apple Pandowdy, 128
  Baked Apples, 138
  Berry Cobbler, 130-131
  Berry Fool, 142
  Blueberry Grunt, 134
  Cherry Crunch, 122
  Peach Slump, 132
  Raspberry Buckle, 136
  Raspberry Trifle, 144
  See also specific fruits

Fudge Frosting, 54

G

German Chocolate Cake, 12-13
Gingerbread, 28
  Men, 182
Glaze
  Apricot, 118
  Chocolate, 22-23
  Glossy Chocolate, 56
Glossy Chocolate Glaze, 56
Gold Cake, 14
Graham Cracker Crust, 116
Grasshopper Pie, 94
Grunt, Blueberry, 134

H

Hard Sauce, 158-159
Hermits, 184
Honey Cake, 42

I

Icing. *See* Frosting
Indian Pudding, 156
Iron cooking range, 2-3

K

Key Lime Pie, 108

L

Lattice-Top Sour Cherry Pie, 74-75
Lattice-Top Strawberry Rhubarb Pie, 76
Layer cakes, 3
Leavening for cakes, 2-3
Lemon
  Bars, 190
  Meringue Pie, 106-107

The Crossing Press publishes
a full selection of cookbooks.
To receive our current catalog,
please call TOLL FREE 800/777-1048.